|| श्रीमदभिनवगुप्तप्रणीतम् परमार्थसारम् ||

The Essence of Supreme Reality or The Paramārthasāra of Abhinavagupta

The *Paramārthasāra* of Abhinavagupta is composed in such an easy style as would enable the reader to comprehend the most abstruse doctrines of Trika Shaivism in a manner that would be free from conceptual confusion and logical inconsistency. The text explains profoundly such philosophical and theological themes as would necessarily constitute the core or heart of any serious discussion. The text attempts at clarifying the following doctrinal principles of Trika Shaivism: cosmology (1-9); ontology (10-13); emanation of objectivity (14-22); bondage and liberation (23-33); the metaphysical status of phenomenon (34-38); nature of knowledge (39-46); self-realisation (47-67); the spiritual status of a yogin after self-realisation (68-88); the theory of transformation (89-93); the behavioural pattern of a liberated yogi (94-96); the graduated process of liberation.

Moti Lal Pandit, trained as a theologian and linguist, has been engaged in Indological research for last fifty years. He has published articles as well as books on a vast range of subjects. Initially he began his research in Vedic religion and philosophy. Gradually he shifted his attention towards Buddhism, and, as a result of this shift, he has been successful in publishing a number of books on Buddhist philosophy and history. For the last several years, however, he has been fully engaged in the study of Trika Shaivism of Kashmir. Some of his publications are: *Vedic Hinduism; Essentials of Buddhist Thought; Philosophy of the Upanishads; Śaṁkara's Concept of Reality; Did Marx Kill God; Buddhism in Perspective; Being as Becoming; Towards Transcendence; Śunyata: The Essence of Mahāyāna Spirituality; Buddhism: A Religion of Salvation; Encounter with Buddhism; The Buddhist Theory of Knowledge and Reality; Transcendence and Negation; The Trika Shaivism of Kashmir; The Disclosure of Being; An Introduction to the Philosophy of Trika Shaivism;The Philophical and Practical Aspects Kāśmīra Shaivism,* and *From Dualism to Non-Dualism.*

॥ श्रीमदभिनवगुप्तप्रणीतम् परमार्थसारम् ॥

The Essence of Supreme Reality

Or

The Paramārthasāra of Abhinavagupta

Translated and Commented by

Moti Lal Pandit

Munshiram Manoharlal
Publishers Pvt. Ltd.

ISBN 978-81-215-1355-5
First published 2021

PRINTED IN INDIA
Published by Ashok Jain *for*
Munshiram Manoharlal Publishers Pvt. Ltd.
PO Box 5715, 54 Rani Jhansi Road, New Delhi-110 055, INDIA

www.mrml.online

For My Grand-Daughters
Maitri and Parthavi
Who have, in the midst of lock-down,
inspired me to undertake the composition
of this text.

Contents

	Praface	*ix*
	Introduction	1
1.	Salutation to the Deity	31
2-3.	Introductory Statement	33
4.	Four Divisions (*aṇḍas*)	35
5.	The Enjoyer	37
6-7.	One Manifesting itself as Many	39
8.	The Appearance of Consciousness	42
9.	The Appearance of the Divine	43
10-11.	The Absolute as Paramaśiva	44
12-13.	The Theory of Rflection and the Appearance of Diversity	46
14.	The Pure Emanation	49
15.	The Impure Emanation	51
16-17	Manifestation of Sheaths (*kañcukas*)	53
18.	Discarding of Sheaths	57
19-20	The Senses and the Organs	59
21-22	The Subtle and Gross Elements	62
23-24	Three Veils of Consciousness	64
25.	Ignorance based View	66
26.	The Appearance of the Many	68
27.	Diversity an Apparent Appearance	70
28-31	Two Kinds of Delusion	72
32.	The Four Coverings of Ātman	76
33.	The Removal of Coverings	77
34.	The Revelatory Nature of Consciousness	79
35.	The States of Animation	80
36.	The Everlasting Purity of the Absolute	82
37.	The Psychic Difference among Contingent The Beings	83
38.	The Appearance of God as Diverse	85

39-40.	Dissolution of Delusion	86
41-42.	Dissolution of Diversity	89
43.	The Nature Brahman	91
44.	Brahman as the Source of Phenomena	93
45.	Interior Emanation	94
46.	External Manifestation	96
47-50	The Process of Self-realisation	98
51-52	The Dissolution of Desultory Misery	102
53-54	Karman as the Cause of Rebirth	104
55-56	Dysfucntionality of Karman	106
57-59	Freedom from the Pain of Rebirth	108
60.	Nature of Liberation	111
61.	Moral Life and Liberation	112
62.	Non-Functionality of Karman	114
63.	Impressions as the Cause of Transmigration	115
64-66	Liberation upon the Dissolution of Impressions	116
67.	Non-Fructification of Karman	119
68.	Disengagement from Conceptual Cognition	121
69.	Freedom from Religious Discipline	123
70.	Indifference Towards Sin and Piety	125
71-73	The Nature of the Liberated	127
74-80	The Vows of a Pāśupata *jñānin*	130
81-82	Perfect Unity as Fulfillment	137
83-84	Purity and Impurity	139
85-86	Liberated while Living	142
87-88	Freedom from Adjuncts	144
89-91	Life-Situation at the Time of Death	146
92-93	Rebirth and Liberation	149
94-95	The Behavioural Pattern of a *jñānin*	151
96.	Instant Liberation	153
97.	Graduated Form of Liberation	155
98-102	Delayed Liberation of a Fallen Yogi	156
103.	Merits of the Knowledge of Reality	160
104-105	Diversity an Apparent Appearance	161
	Glossary	163

Preface

Till the beginning of last century hardly anyone knew that there exists a well-developed philosophical school of thought known as Kashmir Shaivism. With the establishment of Kashmir Sanskrit Series Texts in the beginning of last century, a number of important Sanskrit texts on Shaivism were published, and accordingly people at large came to know about the existence of Kashmir Shaivism. For this act of establishing the Research Center as well as the undertaking of publication of important texts on Kashmir Shaivism, we have to be grateful to Swāmī Rāmajī who inspired the then Mahārāja Pratāp Singh in such a manner as would result in the establishment of this important institution. The Mahārāja Pratāp Singh also deserves our humble gratitude for initiating a programme in terms of which revival of Kashmir Shaivism would become a possibility. It is these two noble souls who initially made the revival of Kashmir Shaivism a possible project. It is around this time that Grierson also published the *Sayings of Lallā,* thereby facilitating the passage for the emergence of knowledge concerning Kashmir Shaivism that would have universal audience.

Insofar as the term Kashmir Shaivism is concerned, it owes its existence to a book, called *Kashmir Shaivism,* written by J.C. Chaterjee who was the first Superintendent of the Research Institute established by the then Mahārāja of Jammu and Kashmir. The traditional nomenclatures by which Kashmir Shaivism is known are Parādvaitavāda, Svātantrayavāda, Rahasyavāda, etc. Also in the *Sarvadarśana-saṁgrha* of Madhvācārya Kashmir Shaivism is simply refereed to as the Pratyabhijñādarśana. All these different nomenclatures have been brought by Abhinavagupta under the rubric of Trika. Thus Kashmir Shaivism is known either as Kashmir Shaivism or as Trika Shaivism. Also it was during the middle of the last century that two prominent scholars, namely, Gopīnātha Kavirāja and K.C. Pandey, made Kashmir Shaivism known to a wider audience through their scholarly publications. Apart these two scholars, Swāmī Lakṣamanjoo also has played an important role in the revival of Kashmir Shaivism. Many Europen and Indian scholars learnt the most secret aspects of Shaivism from him. Also mention must be made of Dr. Baljīnāth Pandit, who composed many original works like, for example, *Svātantrya-darpaṇa* as well as the commentary on the *Śivasūtras.* During the last part of the last century many European scholars have published mumerous texts, and accordingly the essential message of Kashmir Shaivism has reached the public at large. We must not forget to mention the name of Shri Jaideva Singh who, through his many publications, has popularised the teaching of Trika among the masses. He has translated some of the most important texts into English like the *Śivasūtras, Spandakārikās, Pratyabhijñāhṛdayam,* etc. However still the large corpus of Sanskrit texts have neither been edited properly nor published. Lot of effort has to be made to delve deeper into the mysterious world of Kashmir Shaivism.

One of the reasons as to why Kashmir Shaivism has remained a closed book to people outside Kasmhir could be the very physical features of the valley. The high mountains and the difficult terrain must have proved to be one of the major obstructions in the spread of the metaphysical doctrines of Kashmir Shaivism. The second reason could be the harsh Muslim rule, which not only caused destruction to the ancient heritage, but created such obstacles as would become difficult to engage in knowledge-oriented pursuits. As a result of these obstacles nothing much was written except few exceptions. It is important to note at this point that our Gurus, viz., Purohitas, were responsible, to a large extent, in preserving the Sanskrit language as well as the Shāradā script. Had they not secretly preserved the valuable manuscripts, we would have been completely deprived of Sanskrit language, Shāradā script as well as the treasure of manuscripts. Even in the midst of this strenuous effort towards the preservation of our cultural heritage, lot of valuable literary and philosophical texts have been lost forever. We know about these lost texts only through quotations and references. Many important works of Somānanda, Utpaladeva and Abhinavagupta are no more available. We must, thus, express our gratitude to our Purohitas for preserving, under harsh conditions, the rich heritage of which we all are proud. The harshness of Muslim rule can be gauged from the fact that from Yogarāja to Sāhib Kaula, which is to say approximately four hundred years, the number of thinkers that the community produced is muniscule. The last Shaiva thinker of some significance was Harabhaṭṭa Śāstrī, who composed a valuable commentary on the *Pañcasatavī.* This explanation tells us as to why Kashmir Shaivism, even in the valley, had to go underground, which means that it was not possible in such conditions to engage in the activity of spreading the message of Trika Shaivism to public at large. The other reason that could be seen to be responsible in prevenenting the spread of knowledge with regard to Kashmir Shaivism could be the dearth of such text that would introduce the beginner to the rich mysteries of Trika. In the case of the Advaita Vedānta such situation does not prevail. They are fortunate in having a plethora of such texts which have been made as the basis of teachings for the beginners. Trika Shaivism, however, lacks such texts that could be used as tools for teaching the beginners. This lacuna is being, to some extent, bridged by the *Paramārthasāra.* May be it is with such an intention that Abhinavagupta re-casted and re-edited the Vaiṣṇava *Paramārthasāra* of Patañjali in such a manner as would serve his purpose and in terms of which the doctrines of the Trika could be formulated for the beginners. The other text that has been written for the beginners is the *Paraprāveśakā* or *The Entrance into the Absolute* of Kṣemarāja. Apart from these two manograpphs nothing worthwhile exits for the beginners.

Since most people do not have the knowledge of Sanskrit language, so the need for an English translation arose. The translation has been made in such manner as would make it easier to approach the text with an easeful mind. I hope and pray for its success. As to whethr I have succeeded in my mission or not would be known only when it is read by people for whom it is written. At this point I must express my gratitude to my granddaughter, Maitri Pandit, for helping me in editing the text. Lastly. I must express my thanks to the publishers, namely, Munshiram Manoharlal, for undertaking the publication of the *Paramārthasāra*.

Moti Lal Pandit
New Delhi

Introduction

Early to the *Paramārthasāra* of Abhinavagupta, there existed a Vaiṣṇava text of the same name whose authorship has been ascribed to Ādiśeṣa. This Ādiśeṣa, with the passage of time, has been identified with Patañjali, who is considered to be the incarnation of a thousand-headed snake deity, known as Śeṣanāga. As to why Patañjali has been identified with a thousand-headed snake needs some explanation. Such identification may have occurred due to the preponderance of the Nāga cult at the time when the pre-Abhinavagupta *Paramārthasāra* was being composed. The other reason that could be envisaged would be that the author of the text is seen to be possessing such power of thinking as would a thousand-headed snake. It would indicate that the author's intelligence was as sharp as is the edge of a rozor.

There is a belief making rounds that the earlier *Paramārthasāra* represented Sāṁkhya system of thought, and this commonly-held belief owes its existence to Yogarāja, the commentator of the *Paramārthasār* of Abhinavagupta. There is no doubt that the text possesses some elements of the Sāṁkhya system, but when studied in its entirety, it becomes clear that the text is a Vaiṣṇava work. As such it is Vaiṣṇava theism that dominates the thought of the *Paramārthasāra* of Śeṣa.

There are many works or texts of various schools of thought that contain some elements of Sāṁkhya thinking—and that does not mean that the text pertains to the Sāṁkhya system. The Sāṁkhya being the earliest philosophical system, it is but natural to see its influence prevalent everywhere, and thus the Sāṁkhya philosophical terms are found to be present as much in the

Vaiṣṇavism of Mahābhārata as much as they can be located in the Vedāntic theism of the Upaniṣads. Even though the Sāṁkhya elements may have deeply influenced the thinking of Śeṣa, yet it cannot be denied that the work is definitely a Vaiṣṇava in character and thinking. Although Vaiṣṇava in its orientation and content, the philosophical direction of the text embodies such an ontlogy as would be totally representing the metaphysical absolutism. The Vaiṣṇavism of Śeṣa/Patañjali differs redicaly from the Vaiṣṇavism that is more inclined towards the mysticism of myth than reason. Insofar as Patañjali's Vaiṣṇavism is concerned, it is more metaphysical and rational. He develops the superstructure of metaphysical absolutism on sound logical principles.

Whether it be Rāmānuja or Vallabha, the Vaiṣṇava thinkers have a tendency to so wrap their philosophical thinking as to obliterate the difference that exists between reason and emotion. The qualified non-dualism of Rāmānuja or the Viśuddhādvaita of Vallabha may be having a sound philosophical reasoning as its base, yet, on account of intensive devotionalism, it ultimately takes shelter in such emotional forms of thinking as would erode its metaphysical thinking. Insofar as Patañjali is concerned, he sticks to his philosophical worldview like a rock. The non-dualism of Patañjali is as theistic as would enable it to avoid the pitfalls of *vivartavāda* of Śaṁkara. It is, therefore, reasonable to assert that the most ancient Vaiṣṇava form of theistic absolutism is to be found in the *Paramārthasāra* of Patañjali.

It is the *Paramārthasāra* of Ādiśeṣa/Patañjali that became the basis for the text that Abhinavagupta composed. The style, content and the method of presentation of Ādiśeṣa seems to have so much attracted Abhinavagupta as would incline him to adopt this, after necessary editing, as his own. Abhinava made such necessary changes in the original *Paramārthasār* which he deemed fit for the purpose of making a good presentation for the framework of the Trika Śaivism of Kashmir. The intention of adopting this text as his own was simply to present, in simple and lucid language, the philosophical and theological thinking of Trika in such a manner as would be appropriate for the beginner. While re-casting the text, Abhinava avoids discussion on such philosophical topics that are contentious. The purpose is to present Trika Śaivism in such a manner as would be simple and shorn of philosophical rivalry or antagonism. The simplicity of presentation indicates that the use of dry logic evidently becomes unnecessary. Sophisticated logical discussion is to be found in such works as, for example, the *Śivadṛṣṭi* of Somānanda or the *Īśvarapratyabhijñā-kārikā* of Utpalācārya. The *Paramārthasāra* is composed in such a manner as would encompass, in a diction that is simple, the entirety of Trika Śaivism. It is the best available text insofar as the beginner is concerned. One who studies this text with a focused mind will be able to undertake the study of such philosophically sophisticated works as the *Śivadṛṣṭi.*

The themes that Abhinavagputa deals with in the *Paramārthasāra* are both metaphysical and theological. The philosophical themes that are analysed pertain to the description of the Absolute, the nature of causation, the nature of knowledge, the process of manifestation of phenomena, and so accordingly both ontological and epistemological questions are taken into consideration. Insofar as the theological themes are concerned, they are such as would concern themselves with the problem of transmigration, bondage, release from bondage, the methods that facilitate the realisation of freedom from bondage, and the status of a released person.

The text of the *Paramārthasāra* has a commentary of Yogarāja, who was a disciple of Kṣemarāja, and Kṣemarāja himself was the disciple of the great Ācārya Abhinavagupta, which means that Yogarāja was a grand disciple of Abhinavagupta. The commentary of Yogarāja is quite valuable in throwing light on some subtle aspects of Trika Shaivism. It discusses each verse at length, and thereby makes it easier to understand the text. The *Paramārthasāra* of Abhinavagupta, with the passage of time, gained so much popularity among the people with an academic mind that the original text of Ādiśeṣa was quite forgotten. However, some academicians like the grammarian Nāgeśa Bhaṭṭa do quote the *Paramārthasāra* of Ādiśesa, but such is not the rule but an exception. However, it was the *Paramārthasāra* of Abhinavagupta that was popular among the thinkers of the time. There are authors like Maheśvarānanda, the author of *Mahārthamañjarī,* who have referred to it as the *Paramārthasārasaṁgraha.* Likewise Amṛtānanda, too, refers to it with this nomenclature in his *Yoginihṛdaya-dīpikā.* The first English translation of the text that appeared in the Journal of Royal Asiatic Society (1910) was that of L.D. Barnett. It was simply a literal translation of the text devoid of explanation. The translated text was never published as a book, and so remained simply in the form of a published article.

Insofar as the publication of the Sanskrit text of the *Paramārthasāra,* along with its commentary by Yogarāja, is concerned, it was, for the first time, published in the year of 1916 at Srinagar under the rubric called *Kashmir Series of Texts and Studies.* It was republished, with an additional commentary of D.N. Śāstrī in 1981, by Ranvira Kendriya Sanskrit Vidyapeetha, Jammu. Also the text of the *Paramārthasāra* was published by the Īśvara Āshram Trust, Srinagar, in 1977, with a Hindi translation of Sādhikā Prabhadevī, disciple of Swāmī Lakṣmaṇa Joo.

The present English translation along with a brief commentary is so devised as to be helpful and useful to those who are desirous of entering into the virgin field of exploration of what is known as Trika Shaivism of Kashmir. Proper care has been taken in maintaining the philosophical integrity of terms that have metaphysical or theological bearing. The originality of technical terms must never be lost in the process of translation. This translation, while maintaining the integrity of the philosophical and theological ideas of Trika, empowers the seeker in such a manner as would enable him to comprehend the complex philosophical/theological thinking of such texts as the *Śivadṛṣṭi* and the *Īśvarapratyabhijñā-kārikā.*

It is asserted that the ancestors of Abhinavagupta hailed from an area that lies between Gangā and Yamunā. It was king

Lalitāditya, the king of Kashmir, who is said to have invited Atrigupta, the ancestor of Abhinavagupta, to Kashmir. He was provided large tracts of land as well as a residential home at Pravarasenapura near the Sītāmśumauli temple on the banks of the Vitastā. As to the exact location of the temple nothing definite is known on account of the destruction caused by the Muslim rulers of temples. There is a running tradition among Kashmiri Pandits which maintains that the ancestral home of Abhinavagupta was at Gotapura (Guptapura), which lies in the northern outskirts of Srinagar near what is now called Lal Bazar. It is possible that places like Gopītīrtha or Guptatīrtha, which lies on the banks of Dal Lake, may have had some connection with Abhinavagupta. Abhinavagupta, thus, hails from a family of scholars who were invited by the king in the eighths century to settle in Kashmir. Insofar as Abhinava's time is concerned, he is said to have lived during the later part of the tenth century and the earlier part of the eleventh century—and this he himself has attested by giving the dates of composition of the *Kramastotra, Bhairavastotra,* and *Īśvarapratyabhijñā-vivṛti-vimarśinī* as being AD 990,992 and 1014 respectively.

As to what kind of a person Abhinavagupta was is best described in the *Gurunāthaparāmarśa* of Madhurāja. Madhurāja hailed from Kerala, and is said to have travelled from Kerala to Kashmir to be initiated and instructed by Abhinavagupta himself. Madhurāja informs us that Abhinavagupta was so aesthetically inclined as to be a prince, which is to say that he lived in the midst of beauty and enjoyed comfort as a natural mode of life. He seems to have disliked such a mode of life that was characterised by the poverty of a renunciate. The practice of poverty, according to Abhinavagupta, denoted such deprivation of mind and body which is painful and injurious. As Abhinavagupta was not married, so accordingly he neither had a wife nor children, which he himself confirms thus, *ājanma-dāra-suta-bandhu-kathāmanāptaḥ.*

Although unmarried, Abhinavagupta lived in his ancestral home along with his five cousins. As all his cousins were his disciples, so accordingly he taught them the intricate Tantric doctrines and the complex logical arguments of Pratyabhijñā philosophy. One of his disciples, whom he loved much, was his own younger brother, namely, Monorathagupta. It is in the home of a loving disciple, namely, Mandra, where the text of the *Tantrāloka* was composed. Another disciple upon whom Abhinava seems to have showered his unbounded love is Karṇa, who has been mentioned in more than one work. He seems to have lived and worked among his close relatives where the familial care and love seems to have provided the necessary impetus for his creative activity.

Most of the Trika thinkers seem to have preferred the life of a householder. None of the leading lights of this tradition have recommended the cultivation of renunciation as a *sine qua non* for religious life like the Jainas, the Buddhists, the Pāśupstas or the Vedāntins. All the saintly persons seem to have lived a life of a householder, cultivated the social norms in accordance with the rules of the Dharmaśāstra. They seem to have followed with conviction all the necessary rites of passage that pertain to a Brāhmaṇic way of life. Though followers of Tāntric thought and practice, they did not like the Jainas and the Buddhists disturb the social normatives of life. Deeply influenced by Tāntricism, these Trika thinkers would not subscribe to a way of life that was characterised by puritanical thinking.

The Trika Shaivism, while fully Tāntric in its orientation, does not at all discount the cultivation of Vedic way of life. It recognises the necessity of the Vedic way of life for the maintenance of social order. Insofar as the validity of other ways of life are concerned, it accepts them as being valid to the extent they have the capacity of liberating people from the fetters of bondage. It asserts that these paths, whether they be Vedic or non-Vedic, Śrāmaṇic or Brāhmaṇic, have a kind of half-way spirituality, which is to say that these paths may lead to a partial state of liberation. The Buddhists or the Jainas, for example, cannot go higher than the subject of the state of awareness devoid of activity, which in the language of Trika is equated with Vijñānākala.

The Trika Shaivism, while accepting the Vedic way as being valid, follows the Tāntric path insofar as spirituality is concerned, or should way that it has devised such spiritual paths as would terminate in the realisation of liberation from bondage through the non-dual experience of the Absolute. It, therefore, has prescribed definite ways or paths of liberation, which have been so devised as to suit every psychological type. Thus we have the Limited Path, called, *āṇavopāya,* which suits those who are beginners, or who have not yet developed spiritually. For the people who have an intellectual bent of mind, it is the Path of Energy, or *śāktopāya,* that is prescribed. Those who are quite advanced spiritually, it is the Path of Śiva, or the *śāmbhavopāya,* that is prescribed. Accordingly is prescribed the Null Path, or the *an-upāya,* for them who are under deep influence of divine grace (*tīvara-śaktipāta*). All these paths of *sādhanā* are completely Tāntric in nature.

The Trika system of *sādhanā* does not wholly accept the Patañjali system of eight-stepped yoga. It discourages the use of such forms of breath control that, in one way or the other, inflicts pain. It believes in the practice of such forms of yoga that are natural, which is to say that it believes that the flow of practice should be like the free-flow of water in a stream. While analysing the states of consciousness, it asserts that the real revelation of the nature of Being occurs in what it calls the Fourth or Beyond the Fourth. The experience that eventuates in the Fourth is that of immersion (*samāveśa*), which is quite different from the yogic *samādhi*. The *nirvikalpa-samādhi,* though devoid of thoughts, does not embody an experience that is positive, whereas immersion in the ocean of the Absolute is characterised by bliss, and so contains within itself such a reference that is affirmative and in terms of which joy of existence in the from of consciousness is experienced. It is this affirmation of existence in the from "I am" that constitutes the core of immersion as transcendence.

The methods of *sādhanā* that the Trika advocates are deeply grounded in the Tāntric worldview, which is to say that the nature of spiritual practices is such as would express the basic character of Tāntricism. The spiritual methods that the Trika follows have been explored by the Siddhas, which is to say by such persons who have attained every kind of spiritual perfection. These spiritual methods of the Siddhas are so devised as to be easeful, giving rise to quick results in terms of such experinces that are tasteful on account of them being blissful, non-dual, and so expansive as to be infinite. Through the practice of these spiritual exercises the *sādhaka* realises his essential nature as being full of sport, nondifferent from the Absolute.

The aim of the Trika spirituality is to enable the adept to have the recognition (*pratyabhijñā*) of one's essential nature in terms of which the self is recognised as being a mass of consciousness-bliss. This self-recognition as being consciousness-bliss can be realised while one is still living in the world of space-time. As followers of Tāntricism, the Trika Siddhas discouraged such ascetical practices that verged on the torture of the body. It also discounted such violent (*haṭha*) practices as the school of Haṭhayoga prescribes. The method of suppressing the emergence of the waves in the mind, as prescribed by the classical school of yoga, is not encouraged, as such a practice could lead to mental derangement. Instead of suppression, Trika advises that these waves of emotions should be allowed to come upon the surface of the ocean, called mind, so that their thinning occurs in a natural way. Instead of suppression, Trika prescribes such Tāntric ways that are so easeful as to be spontaneous (*sahaja*), and accordingly the adept is enabled to realise intuitively his divine nature as being non-different from Paramaśiva. Through this spiritual realisation the adept comes to know that this contracted individual is none else than Śiva itself who, out of his own free will, assumes the role of a finite being. In other words, the entirety of phenomena is but the self-expansion of Śiva itself. To put it in philosophical terms, it would mean that the universe is but the congealing of the Universal Consciousness (*citi*) itself. The very unfolding of the universe denotes the contraction of the Divine, and its dissolution indicates the expansion of Śiva.

There is a school of thought, inspired largely by western orientalism, which equates Tāntricism with subversion, rebellion and with antinomian tendencies. Such characterization of Tāntricism does not represent the essence of truth. There could be some aspects of Tāntricism which may, on the surface level, seem to be opposing the Vedic view of life. However, the so-called antinomian practices of Tāntricism really are a new way of looking at truth, which is to say that the Tāntric *sādhanā,* being experimental in nature, has added new perspective to the fund of knowledge that was represented by the Vedic view. Therefore, it is erroneous to assume that Tāntricism, in contrast to Vedism, stands on the opposite pole. Instead of bifurcating Tāntricism from Vedism in terms of opposition or contrast, we should see to it as a further extension of Vedism in terms of which spirituality is contextualised appropriately to the needs of the prevailing situation. It is not possible to practice spirituality these days in the manner it used to be practiced five hundred years ago. It is the prevailing situation that by itself inserts change in our way of life. Thus it is the prevailing situation that forces us to contextualise our mode of thinking appropriately. The emergence of Tāntricism accordingly has to be seen as an attempt at contextualising the Vedic religious way of life, and Tāntricism has fruitfully accomplished this task. What was previously thought to be a prohibited practice doctrinally is now given a new lease of life by having a hermeneutic which abolishes the distinction between purity and impurity. Since Tāntricism sees every aspect of phenomena as being the extension of the Divine, so accordingly nothing is pure or impure for it; rather every phenomenon is bristling with the Divine pulsation. Whatever distinctions or differences may exist, they are mental rather than real. Tāntricism, while having a non-dualistic view of Reality, does not recognise difference between the two contrasting images as being real. The seemingly contrasting difference is subsumed under the reubric of non-duality. The so-called external diversity exists to the extent non-dual nature of Reality remains unrecognised. Difference of diversity vanishes the moment unitary nature of Reality is recognised, and so the dialectical difference, which is the bane of empirical thinking, disappears in the ocean of the Divine when everything is experienced as having been immersed in it.

It should be clear by now that the emergence of Tāntricism did not take place on account of the conflict with the Vedic way of life; rather it should be seen as a contextual extension of the existing fund of knowledge to serve appropriately the exigencies of time. It becomes quite clear when the Shaivas of Kashmir did not establish distinctively a separate sect, but rather inserted Tāntric thinking and practices gently into the over-all Vedic way of life without disturbing the social life. While following such Tāntric practices that had a strong soteriological orientation, the Trika Shaivas simultaneously adhered to such normative behaviour as was prescribed by the Dharmaśāstras and the Smṛtis. One of the effects of Tāntric contextualisation into the text of Vedism resulted in the abolishing of caste distinctions insofar as interiorisation of spirituality is concerned. As a result of this contextualization, Abhinavagupta, in his *Tantrāloka*, could go so far as to assert that a knowledgeable socalled caṇḍāla should be preferred to be one's guru than an ignoble Brāhmaṇa. Also dignity to women was restored in terms of which she was equated to the mouth of Śiva. A guru, so it is said, could not impart initiation unless accompanied by his female companion. A woman could also be a guru provided she had the required knowledge of the scriptures. In this manner the religious thinking of people was so contextualised as would meet the requirements of the prevailing situation. The assertion of the orientalists with regard to Tāntricism as being subversive is completely demolished when interpreted within the framework of contextualistion of the emerging knowledge. The Trika thinkers were far ahead of their times when the removal of caste distinction and restoration of dignity to woman was inserted into the existing religious and social behaviour. The Trika thinkers have taught us that violence as a response to social problems is not a solution; rather solution lies in such a response that is skillful and rooted in wisdom. This openness of Trika is quite visible when every kind of restriction has been removed with regard to the sacred initiation in the spiritual path of Shaivism. Anyone can be initiated provided he/she is possessed by deep faith in, and devotion to, Paramaśiva. In this manner knowledge and devotion have been so intermingled as would make it sweet and enjoyable. The Trika thinkers have sprinkled the path of spirituality with the blissful droplets of ambrosia. A clear and balanced approach to logic and emotion is maintatined in such a manner as would result in viewing both of them as being complimentary. Insofar as the sensual enjoyment is concerned, the Trika does not object to it. The sensual enjoyment, rather, is seen as a precursor to the experience of the divine delight. From the sensual joy to the supreme delight the adept makes his spiritual journey in a graduated manner whereby he ascends higher scales of enstasy. It was Abhinavagupta who removed the notion of negation in the over-all philosophical and spiritual framework of Trika. Thus Trika is not a spirituality that is characterised by injuctions and prohibitions.

Yogarāja, who was a disciple of Kṣemarāja, hailed from the village called Vethavottur (Vitastāpurī), which is situated at the foot of the Banihal Mountain, and by the side of which the river Vitastā or Jehlum flows downwards. At this village the Vitastā as personified Goddess is worshipped even now. It is this Yogarāja who wrote a commentary on the *Paramārthasāra* of Abhinavagupta. Kṣemarāja, who was the disciple of Abhinavagupta, was a prolific writer, and composed commentaries on various Āgamic and non-Āgamic texts. Apart from his commentaries, he also wrote some original works such as the *Pratyabhijñāhṛdaya.* Although a disciple of Abhinavagupta, he has not written any commentary on any of the works of his revered guru. So far the scholars have evaluated Trika Shaivism from the perspective of Kṣemarāja. It is time now that the Trika Shaivism be analysed in the light of the teachings of *Paramārthasār.*

There is a tradition running through the scriptural texts that says that the entire gamut of teachings got completely lost due to the vagaries of time. Somehow the teaching were retrieved, and this impossible task was accomplished by sage Durvāsa who, on account of the divine grace, got so inspired as would result in the swelling of an urge within him which would compell him to impart this divine stream of teaching to some deserving disciple, and this worthy disciple was non other than Tryambakāditya. It is through his mind-born son and daughter that the sacred teachings have come down to us through a line of teachers. They established two streams or lines of teachers– one stemming from his daughter, and the other from his son, which are known as the Ardha-Tryambaka-maṭhikā and the Tryambaka-maṭhikā respectively. The former line of teachers centered on Kāṅgara valley, and one of the well- known teachers of this line was Śrī Śambhūnātha, who was the teacher of Abhinavagupta. Abinavagupta highly praises his teacher as being the embodiment of Śiva itself. The other line of teachers that stemmed from his son established itself in the valley of Kashmir, and is known as the Tryambaka-maṭhika. The first fifteen teachers of this line are said to have been mind-born, and the sixteenth teacher, namely, Saṅgmāditya, came to Kashmir in and around 8th century. While visiting Kashmir, he is said to have married a local Brahmin girl, and the progeny that followed him consisted of Varśāditya, Arunāditya, Ānanda and Somānanda. All of them continued the tradition of teaching by being the gurus of maṭhikas. Somānanda, the author of *Śivadṛṣṭi,* was the twentieth member of this lineage.

Simultaneously was occuring the disclosure of Āgamas within the framework of triadic system of thought in terms of ten dualistic Āgamas, eighteen dualistic-cum-non-dualistic Āgamas, and the sixty-four non-dualistic Āgamas. Thus the three streams of thought came into existence which unfolded itself in the form of the establishment of doctrinal dualism (*bhedavāda*) qualified non-daulism (*bhedābhedavāda*) and non-dualism (*abhedavāda*). In the valley of Kashmir it were the non-dualistic Āgamas that were preferred over the texts that were either representing doctrinal dualism or qualified non-dualism. There was a group of texts, six in number (*ṣaḍardha*), which were collective known as *Saura* texts on account of them being as energetic as is the energy of the sun. These texts, on account of their energetic nature, where considered to be possessing higher merit than the sixty-four non-dual Āgamas. Insofar as Trika is concerned, it considered the three *Saura* texts of great importance, namely, the *Siddha-tantra, Vamaka* or *Namaka-tantra,* and the *Mālinī-vijaya-tantra.* The entire gamut of Trika thought and practice is derived from the *Mālinī-vijaya-tantra.* It is the trinity of these texts from which the Trika nomenclature is derived, representing thereby a specific doctrinal school of Shaivism in Kashmir, initiated by Tryambakāditya, and the line of teachers that followed him. Besides these *Saura* texts and the sixty-four Āgamas, the other texts that played an important role in the formation of Trika thought are the *Svacchanda, Netra* and the *Rudrayāmala Tantras.* All these revelatory texts came into being between 700 and 800 AD and accordingly this period is characterised by the creative outflow of philosophical thought which lasted till the of inception of Islam in Kashmir. Coming of Islam proved to be the death-knell of all that that had been achieved in culture, music, literature and philosophy. Apart from the above scriptures that have played a mojor role in the formation and formulation of the Trika, there is another foundational text, namely, the *Śivasūtras,* which has enumerated the basic theological and philosophical concepts of Trika through its aphorisms. With regard to the origin of the text, there are two parallel running traditions, one of which owes its existence to Kṣemarāja. The tradition that Kṣemarāja initiated in his commentary on the *Śivasūtras* runs like this. It is asserted that Śiva appeared in a dream to Vasugupta telling him that he should go to the Mahādeva Mountain where he will find the text of the *Śivasūtras* inscribed on a boulder. As directed by Śiva in the dream, Vasugupta accordingly visited the place indicated in the dream, and he found to his amazement the boulder standing there. He so pushed the boulder as would be possible for it to turn around, and lo, he found the text of the *Śivasūtras* inscribed on the boulder. The other tradition with regard to the origin of the *Śivasūtras* is this. Śiva is said to have appeared to Vasugupta in a dream, and during the dreamperiod the entire text was revealed by Śiva to Vasugupta. Upon coming out of the dream state, Vasugupta remembered the entire text, and accordingly composed the text of the *Śivasūtras*. As to whether we should give any credence to these similar-dissimilar traditions depends upon one's state of mind. What cannot be denied is the authorship of the text, as both the traditions affirm Vasugupta as being the author of the *Śivasūtras*. The text of the *Śivasūtras* seems to have been composed in the early part of the 9th century AD.

Vasugupta was fortunate enough in having a worthy disciple in the person of Kallaṭa Bhaṭṭa, who lived during the reign of Avantivarman, which is to say in the later part of the 9th century AD. He seems to have been spiritually highly evolved, and this fact is affirmed by Kalhaṇa in his *Rājataraṅgiṇī* (V. 66) when he refers to him as having descended from heaven, in the form of a *siddha,* upon the earth. No other Shaiva personage has been referred to so reverentially by Kalhaṇa as is Kallaṭa Bhaṭṭa. Although Somānanda, apart from Kallaṭa, has been mentioned by Kalhaṇa, his mention, however, is more in the context of political upheavals that occurred in Kashmir during this period than for his spiritual or intellectual attainments. Kallaṭa Bhaṭṭa, on the contrary, has been so mentioned as would establish the credibility of his spiritual attainments. The spiritual fame of Kallaṭa was as widespread as would attract people to the Shaiva school of Tryambaka. He composed many original works, most of which have been lost due to the historical upheaval, and are known only through references or quotations. The two most important works of his, namely, the *Spandakārikā* and the *Spandavṛtti,* known jointly as *Spandasarvasva,* are available. Some of his works like the *Svasvabhāva-saṃbodhana* and the *Tattvavicāra* are known only through quotations from these works. One of his important but lost works—. *Tattvārthacintāmaṇi* —has been quoted by many authors extensively. He is said to have composed a commentary on the *Śivasūtra* called *Madhuvāhinī,* which of course is no more available. Thus Kallaṭa seems to have played a major role theoretically and practically in the establishment of Trika school of Shaivism in Kashmir.

The historical period during which Avantivarman ruled Kashmir was such as would allow the bursting forth, at a great speed, the creative impulse in the manner never seen before in the field of art, culture, philosophy and theology. Great literary luminaries emerged during this period, which allowed the free flow of thinking to flow in various directions. It is during this period that Pradyumna Bhaṭṭa, the cousin of Kallaṭa Bhaṭṭa, composed the famous lyrical hymn known as the *Tattvagarbhastotra.* In this lyrical hymn Shāktic tendencies are quite visible, and accordingly much light is thrown on Shaivism from the perspective of Śakti. It is also during this period that the first philosophical text - - - *Śivadṛṣṭi* - - - was composed by Somānanda, the twentieth member of the lineage of Tryambaka. He headed the Tryambaka-maṭhikā, and accordingly gave firm footing to the Tryambaka school of Shaivism in Kashmir through his philosophical composition and teaching. He is also said to have written a very scholarly commentary on the *Parātriṁśaka,* which, however, is no more available. He was fortunate in having an exceptional disciple in the person of Utpaladeva who extended the teaching of his teacher through such a philosophical text as the *Īśvarapratyabhijñā.* It is, besides the *Śivadṛṣṭi,* the most important philsophical text on the non-dualism of the Trika school of Shaivism. He also composed three smaller philosophical treatises jointly known as the *Siddhatrayī,* which have to be seen as serving a kind of supplement to the *Īśvarapratyabhijñā.* He composed commentaries on all these four works of his as well as on the *Śivadṛṣṭi.* These commentaries of Utpaladeva are not available in their full form. What we possess are fragmentas of these commentaries.

He seems to have written some more works, but whose titles are unknown to us. Such an inference is based on the availability of some quotations of his which are not to be found in the existing texts. Apart from being a philosopher-cum-theologian of high merit, he was also an outstanding poet, and this fact is borne out by his composition of the *Śivastotrāvalī,* which as a hymn contains religio-philosophic poetic content of high merit. It is so popular that it is still sung commonly among the Kashmiri Pundit households. Besides Somānanda and Utpaladeva, the other person of repute of this period is Rāmakaṇṭha, the younger brother of the court poet of Avantivarman, namely, Muktākaṇa. Rāmakaṇṭha composed a commentary, called *Spandavivṛtti,* on the *Spandakārikā* of Kallaṭa Bhaṭṭa. He also wote a commentary on the *Bhagavadgītā,* following the Kāśmīrian recension. The other great personage of this period is Bhaṭṭa Nārāyaṇa who composed a lyrical hymn, namely, the *Stvacintāmaṇi,* in praise of Śiva. Thus both philosophical and devotional literature was, during this period, given due attention,which laid down the firm footing for Shaivite superstructure that would later on be built by Abhinavagupta.

The first excellent commentary on the *Śivasūtra—Vārtika—* was composed by Bhāskara Bhaṭṭa who was the seventh teacher of the line that stemmed from Vasugupta. This commentary on the *Śivasūtra* is far more authentic on account of having received knowledge directly from Vasugupta via Kallaṭa Bhaṭṭa down the line of teachers. Most of the teachers of this line were not only philosophers, but were blessed with the realisation of the truth that they were teaching. Also the beauty of this commentary lies in the fact that the author does not engage in unnecessary discussion of irrelevant topics nor does he burden the text with quotations that need not be there. Instead he explains each doctrinal point from the perspective of knowledge that he has received through the chain of teachers. Thus this commentary of Bhāskara is far more authentic than the scholarly commentary of Kṣemarāja. He lived little before Abhinavagupta, and most probably he may be the same Bhāskara whom Abhinava refers as one of his teachers. Around this period also Utpala Vaiṣṇava who, though a follower of Pañcarātra system, was impressed by Shaivite thought in such a manner as would urge him to write a highly prized commentary on the *Spandakārikā,* namely, *Spandapradīpikā.* This commentary of Upala Vaiṣṇava is of great significance on account of it throwing light on some unknown historical facts of Kashmir Shaivism. While composing the commentary, Utpala Vaiṣṇava quotes profusedly from Pañcarātra sources with the intention of elevating the Pañcarātra system to the same elevated level that was enjoyed by the Trika system.

It is from the quotations of Utpala that we come to know about the extinct works of Kallaṭa Bhaṭṭa. Utpala Vaiṣṇva agrees with the assertion that Bhaṭṭa Kallaṭa is considered as the author of the *Spandakārikā*.

In the middle of the tenth century appeared one of the greatest thinker and yogi upon the soil of Kashmir, namely, Ācārya Abhinavagupta. The contribution he made in the field of philosophy, theology, literary criticism and aesthetics is unparalleled. He not only changed the course or trajectory of Trika Shaivism, but elevated it to the highest metaphysical position in such a manner as would enable it to compete with other well-developed metaphysical systems of thought. Prior to the commencement of Abhinavagupta, there were quite a number of lineages who were often at odds with each other, and would accordingly pull in different directions. These lineages were seemingly trying to develop as independent schools of thought. Abhinava, through his genius, put a brake on such alienating tendencies among the various lineages that would have resulted in giving rise to rivalry and to doctrinal disputes. Abhinavagupta so synthesized the doctrinal thinking of these various schools, such as, Pratyabhijiñā, Kaula, Spanda and Krama, as would unify them under the rubric of Trika without damaging the doctrinal thinking that these schools respectively represented. The outstanding originality of his philosophic vision is quite evident in his commentaries. He is said to have composed commentaries on all the major works of Somānanda and Utpaladeva. Although all his philosophical commentaries may not be available, yet two of his major commentaries on the *Īśvarapratyabhijñā* are available. One of them, namely, *Vimarśinī,* is a commentary on the verses of the *Īśvarapratyabhijñā* and the other is the commentary on the *Ṭikā* of Utpala on his own work, which, however, is no more available. Had the *Ṭīkā* been available, it would have proved of great help to students to understand the commentary of Abhinavagupta thoroughly, which is known as the *Īśvarapratyabhijñā-vivṛti-vimarśinī*. The *Īśvarapratyabhijñā* has accordingly enjoyed the status of being the most mature philosophic work of Trika. Insofar as his commentaries on the *Śivadṛṣṭi* of Somānanda and the *Siddhitrayī* of Utpaladeva are concerned, they unfortunately are no more available, which is a great loss to human civilization.

The task that Abhinavagupta undertook of arranging, compiling and interpreting the doctrines and practices of Trika system in the *Tantrāloka* is of gigantic proportions. The text of the *Tantrāloka,* in its *KSST* edition, consists of twelve volumes. In these volumes every doctrinal aspect is expressed, explained and interpreted from both philosophical/theological perspectives. There is no parallel to be found to the *Tantrāloka* in the gamut of philosophical or religious literature of India. The text of the *Tantrāloka* has a very good commentary of Jayaratha, known as the *Viveka.* In the absence of this commentary it would have been quite difficult to understand the text of the *Tantrāloka.* Fortunately we have a very good commentary of Jayaratha which has made our task of approaching the text easier. Realising that very few people would be able to undertake the study of the entire text of the *Tantrāloka,* so Abhinavagupta accordinagly composed an abbreviated version, in the form of *Tantrasāra,* of it, and which has been published in two volumes. The prose of the text is written in such a form as would be simple and easy to comprehend. The commentary, called *Vivaraṇa,* on the *Parātriṁśaka,* is very profound, as it explains the most esoteric and abstruse aspects of Trika yoga in a manner that could be understood with a firm intellectual grip. In addition to the above texts, Abhinavagupta also composed a profound commentary, called *Vārtika,* on the *Mālinī-vijay-tantra.* It would not be wrong to assert that the *Mālinīvijaya-tantra* provides the necessary philosophical/theological framework to the edifice of the Trika. The *Vārtika* is a voluminous work, which is written in simple Sanskrit. The other important work that Abhinavagupta composed is his *Kramakeli,* which is a commentary on the *Kramastotra* of Siddhanātha. The text deals with the philosophical concept of "Kālī" from the perspective of Shāktism. As a poet of high quality, Abhinavagupta has composed a number of hymns which deal both with philosophical and theological issues. One of his popular hymns - - *Bhairavastotra* - -

is still being sung in the Shaiva temples as well homes of the Kashmiri Pandits. He also composed an easy text for the beginners, namely, *Paramārthasāra* and the *Bodhapañcadaśikā.* In the person of Abhinavagupta, Trika embodies the peak of its evolution both philosophically and spiritually. As Śaṁkara is considered to be the ultimate authority concerning Advaita Vedānta, similarly Abhinavagupta is the final authority with regard to the doctrines of Trika.

After Abhinavagupta it was his disciple, Kṣemarāja, who continued the tradition of scholarship through his commentaries and original works. He was a prolific writer and wrote accordingly numerous works on different topics. The philosophic treatise that he composed is known as the *Pratyabhijñāhṛdaya,* which, however, is unable to explain as to what constitutes the essence of the Doctrine of Recognition. Instead of focusing on the philosophic issues raised by the Pratyabhijñā, Kṣemarāja meanders in the by-lanes of scholarship by conducting the discussion on such systems that in no manner belong to the Trika family. He also composed a short but concise treatise for the beginners, which is known as the *Parāprāveśikā,* or *The Entrance into the Supreme.* The commentary that he composed on the *Śivasūtra,* namely, the *Vimarśinī,* is, no doubt, scholarly, but suffers from the lack of clarity of expression due to the excessive use of quotations. While quoting from various sources, Kṣemarāja does not make an effort at explaining their relevance and meaning in the context of the *sūtra.* The exegesis of Kṣemarāja of the text becomes clear only when we study the commentary-*Śivasūtravārtika* - of his disciple, Varadarāja. The interpretation of the *Śivasūtra* of Bhaṭṭa Bhāskara is far more convincing than the one offered by Kṣemarāja. Another work of scholarly standing is his commentary on the *Spandakārikā,* namely, the *Spandanirṇaya.* He also composed another commentary on the first verse of *Spandakārikā,* namely, the *Spandasandoha,* which attempts to explain the doctrine of pulsation (*spanda*). He also composed commentaries on the devotional texts of Utpaladeva's *Śivastotrāvalī* and Bhaṭṭa Nārāyaṇa's *Stvacintāmaṇi.* He wrote commentaries on some of the Tāntric texts like the *Netra-tantra* and the *Svacchanda-tantra.* He is said to have written a commentary on the *Vijñānabhairava,* which is no more available. However, it was Śivopadhyāya of seventeenth century who has written a compact and scholarly commentary on the *Vijñānabhairava.* Alongside Kṣemarāja, there emerged another luminary who enriched the Trika system through his serious scholarship, and this person is none other than Jayaratha of twelfth century. He has rightly and skillfully served the cause of Trika Shaivism by composing a voluminous commentary on the *Tantrāloka.* In the absence of this commentary, it would have been very difficult to understand the complexity of thought of the text. The commentary not only explains the abstruse currents of thought of the *Tantrāloka,* but is a treasure-house of quotations from many unavailable Tāntric texts. It also throws a lot of light with regard to the historical evolution of Shaivism in Kashmir.

There were quite a number of Shaiva thinkers who, while pursuing their supiritual goal of selfrealisation, adopted such an interpretive view of Reality as would enhance the acceptability of Shākta point of view. One of the foremost thinkers of this line of thinking was Pradyumna Bhaṭṭa who extolled the Shāktic conception of Reality in his famous lyrical hymn, namely, *Tattvagarbhastotra.* In addition to Pradyumn Bhaṭṭa, there were thinkers like Amṛtānanda and Punyānanda who were responsible in giving philosophic status to the concept of Reality as being of the nature of Energy. A specific tradition of Shāktism was started around the 8th century by Śivānandanātha, and this Shāktic tradition is known as the Way of Kālī, which is to say, Kālīnaya. It is a complex and sophisticated method of the Yoga of Knowledge *(jñāna-yoga).* Fundamental doctrinal principle of this tradition pertain to the worship of Kālī, which is seen as representing the metaphysical divine power of the Absolute, and this divine power is classified as being of twelve types. Thus the twelve Kālīs represent the twelve aspects of divine power of the Absolute, which is mentally so meditated upon as would result in the realisation of unity with the divine power of the Absolute. There is a tendency among some scholars to treat it as an independent school, and this view has received impetus from Jayaratha who refers to Kālīnaya as Kramadarśana. However Abhinavagupta looks upon it as a special kind of *śāktopāya*, and so accordingly he has included it into the over-all system of the Trika yoga. The doctrinal teaching of Kālīnaya were transmitted by Śivānandanātha to his three female disciples, namely, Keyūravatī, Madanikā and Kālyanikā. Abhinavagupta received the teachings of this Shāktic tradition from Ujjaṭa and Udbhaṭṭa and it seems that this line of teachers has its source in Madanikā. The main disciples of these three female teachers were Govindarāja, Bhānukācārya and Erakanātha. The lines of teachers that stemmed from Govindarāja and Bhānukācārya seem to have gained considerable acceptance among the people. Govindarāja is said to have initiated Somānanda into the system of Kālīnaya, and from Somānanda through a long line of teachers it reached to Jayaratha. The line of teachers that stemmed from Bhānuka was responsible in imparting the knowledge of the Kālīnaya to Abhinavagupta. The Kālīnaya seems to have gained such widespread popularity among the people as would lead Jayaratha to maintain it to be an independent school of thought. In the far south appeared a saint-scholar of high repute in the person of Maheśvarānanda/ Gorakṣañatha who, though a Kaula in practice, maintained a Shāktic point of view with regard to Reality. He composed a philosophical work called *Mahārthamañjarī* as well as a commentary on it, namely, the *Parimal.* A Tāntric treatise of significance, namely, the *Kāma-kalā-vilāsa* was composed by Puṇyānanda, which has been commented upon by Amṛtānanda. He also wrote a detailed commentary–*Cidvilāsa*–on the *Yognīhṛdaya*. A teacher in Kaulism, namely, Śitikaṇaṭha of thirteenth century, wrote in old Kashmirian language *Mahānayaprakāśa.* Another author of repute on Kaulism is Sāḥib-Kaula of seventeenth century. He wrote many wonderful Shāktic works, and one of the popular works of his is *Devīnāmavilāsa.*

It would be quite erroneous to think that Shaiva and Shākta views are so independent views of Reality as to represent two opposite schools of thought. The Shaiva and Shākta views, however, are so interwoven with each other as would not allow them to disentangle themselves from each other. As Śiva cannot be conceived apart from Shakti, likewise to think of Shakti apart from Śiva would be a grave mistake. Is it possible for us to separate warmth or luminosity from fire? The answer would be that it is not possible, because it is the intrinsic nature of fire to be both warm and luminous. The difference, if there is any, between the two systems lies on emphasis, which is to say that the Shaivites put more emphasis on the consciousness aspect, whereas the Shāktas lay emphasis upon the energy aspect. It would, thus, indicate that the Shaivas have an abstract view of Reality, whereas Shāktas are more practical in their approach to Reality. Since the Absolute is single and non-dual, there can be no divisibility in the nature of Reality. The approach to Reality from two perspectives is possible, and that is what the Shaiva-Shākta approaches represent. The Absolute as I-consciousness is transcendent to both mental and physical phenomena. It cannot be circumscribed by any form of causality. It is accordingly spoken of as being beyond the physical and mental realms. The Absolute shines in every phenomena, and it is on account of this shining that every phenomenon shines or becomes manifest. The Absolute as I-consciousness is alwayas aware of its Godhead, and accordingly it tends to manifest itself outwardly as external phenomena. This tendency of the Absolute as Godhead gives rise to the manifestation of divine activities in terms of emanation, preservation, dissolution, concealment and revelation. The Absolute may be said to be Śiva in its transcendent aspect, but Shakti when viewed immanently. It is through Shakti that all the five divine activities of emanation, preservation, dissolution, concealment and revelation of the Absolute Godhead are carried out. It would not be wrong to assume that Shaivas lay more emphasis on philosophical theories, whereas Shāktas are more practical, and so are prone to engage themselves in practical *sādhanā*.

It should be by now clear that Shāktism and Shaivism are not parallel, contrasting and opposing philosophical schools. They represent, instead, the same philosophical truth with a difference of emphasis. The Shāktas see ultimate reality in terms of energy, whereas the Shaivas give emphasis on the consciousness aspect of reality. The realisation of ultimate truth happens in terms of both consciousness and energy, which is to say that the non-dual Absolute embodies in itself both consciousness and energy and it is, in the language of Pratyabhijñā, spoken of as *prakāśa* and *vimarśa*. Shāktism, without any demur, accepts all the philosophical ideas of Shaivism, whereas the Shaiva teachers have wholeheartedly embraced Shāktic spiritual practices as a means of realising the highest truth. It would mean that Shaivism and Shāktism have to be viewed as representing the two aspects of the same and identical truth, which is Paramaśiva as being both conscriousness and energy. Some of the great thinkers of the tradition have been as syncretistic as to syncronise both aspects in such a manner as would actualise the disappearance of the opposing views. Thus Kallaṭa Bhaṭṭa, Somānanda and Abhinavagupta were syncretistic in their approach, and accordingly eliminated any kind of difference that may have cropped up between Shaivism and Shāktism. It is in this context of unity that Pradyumna Bhaṭṭa, a Shākta philosopher, has been mentioned by Utpaladeva as a being a Shaiva. Thus you find a galaxy of authors like Śivānandanātha, Maheśvarānanda and Sāhib Kaul who were both Shaivas/Shāktas. It is, however, Lallā who represents this synthetic religio-philosophical spirituality at its best, and in terms of which she gave expression to it through her lyrical poetry in Kashmiri language.

It was Abhinavagupta through whose genius Trika Shaivism bloomed like a lotus in terms of which perfect syncretisation was affected between Shaivism and Shāktism. For Abhinava Paramaśiva is the philosophic Absolute in its transcendent (*anuttara*) aspect, and it is this very Absolute that is seen as assuming the role of Godhead in its immanent aspect. Thus Paramaśiva is both metaphysical Absolute and a theistic God, which means that both the philosophical and religious requirements are thereby fulfilled. While giving firm philosophical footing to theistic absolutism, Abhinava thereby is affirming a conception of Reality which is not, like the *brahman* of Śaṁkara, so peaceful as to be devoid of awareness/activity. The Absolute of Śaṁkara is definitely endowed with the light of consciousness, but is deviod of awareness, which is to say that It does not know itself as being of the nature of light. It is like saying that a diamond is full of light, but is not at all alware of its luminosity. This non-awareness of being of the nature of light would indicate that the *brahman* of Śaṁkara is as inert as is a luminous diamond. Instead of inert *brahman,* Abhinavagupta is in favour of such an Absolute who not only is of the nature of light, but consists of full of awareness, which is to say that the Absolute as Godhead is fully aware of its nature as being the light. The Absolute as I-consciousness is said to be consisting of *prakāśa* and *vimarśa,* which is equated with the light of consciousness and awareness. The Absolute, in the language of theology, is seen to be pulsating or vibrating within itself constantly. It is the pulsation of the Absolute as consciousness that embodies its Godhead, and accordingly are reflected its five processes or powers in terms of which emanation, preservation, resorption, concealment and revelation eventuate. The Absolute in its transcendent aspect is beyond the reach of mind, intellect and speech. We apprehend the Absolute through its immanent aspect, particularly when displaying the sport of manifestation of categories. It is the basic nature of the Absolute as Godhead to engage in the activity of the manifestation of categories. When the Absolute is referred to as I-consciousness, it should not be interpreted in terms of a psycho-physical construct called ego, but as pure self-awareness. The eternity and infinity of the Absolute indicates the fact that It is beyond the conditioning processes of space and time. Its unconditioned nature can be expressed only through such terms as infinity and eternity. As absolutely free and sovereign, the Absolute is completely free from the determinate factors of causality, which means that it is not dependent on anything except itself. The manifestation of categories, thus, is the outcome of Its own free will, and the power of independent will initiates the process of both manifestation and resorption. Whatever activities the Absolute as Godhead undertakes, they are all the outcome of its own free will.

The Trika concept of the Absolute is such as would do justice to the Shāktic view of reality as being dynamic, which, in theological terms, is called pulsation/energy, thereby denoting constant throbbing of absolute consciousness. The Shaiva view of the Absolute as being pure and infinite I-consciousness represents the static view, and so in totality the Trika view of the Absolute has to be seen as being the combination of both the Shaiva and Shākta views. When the Absolute reposes in-itself, which denotes the withdrawal of the manifest universe, it represents the indeterminate, and thereby static, state of the Absolute. When, on the other hand, the Absolute as Godhead engages in the five divine processes of emanation, maintenance, resorption, concealment and revelation, it is known as the dynamic aspect of Reality. From this analysis it may be concluded that Śiva, as it were, denotes the fundamental aspect of Reality, whereas Shakti may be seen as embodying his essential nature. The externalisation of manifestation of categories is not eventuated either by the *māyā* of Advaita Vedānta or by the *vāsanās* of Yogācāra, which is to say by the flow of internally stored *vasānās*. It is the very nature of Godhead to allow the spontaneous flow of manifestation to occur. The Absolute Godhead throws out of itself (*vamana)* the entire manifestation from Sādaśiva to Earth category. Whatever is manifested, it is not to be treated as an illusory appearance, as happens in the case of Vedānta of Śaṁkara. Rather the manifestation is to be understood as being the appearance of the Absolute itself. From a relative perspective the appearance of categories is to be recognised as being true, whereas at the absolute level the manifestation of categories is recognised as being non-different from the Absolute. This is how the Trika Shaivism views the manifestation of categories as being the embodiment of the Absolute, and this view of manifestation of categories constitutes one of the main differences from the absolutism of Vedānta.

The impact of Shāktic influence on Shaivism is quite evident when the Absolute is viewed not only as consciousness, but also as bliss, which accordingly indicates the playful nature of Godhead. When the Absolute brims over with bliss, there spontaneously occurs the "sending forth" of objectivity in terms of which the manifestation of phenomenal categories occurs. The divine playfulness of the Absolute Godhead is of such nature as would terminate in the initiation of external movement towards objective manifestation. When the movement for external manifestation is initiated, there occurs no transformation or change within the essential nature of Godhead. The process of manifestation is enacted in such a manner as is a reflection reflected in a mirror, which means that the entire process of external manifestation is reflected as a reflection in the mirror of consciousness. As the reflection does not taint the mirror in any manner, likewise the reflection of the manifestaton of the categories does not taint the mirror of consciousness. Thus the shining of reflection in the psychic mirror of consciousness is to be seen as the self-extension, in the form of the manifestaton of the universe, of Godhead itself, which, in other words, means that the world, for all practical purposes, is the expansion or congealing of the universal consciousness. In this manner it is the absolute Godhead that appears as impure and pure categories as well as in the form of material and mental phenomena. Such occurrence of manifestation of categories is actualised on account of the Absolute being at the same time a theistic God. It is the theistic Absolute that answers rationally the question of causation regarding the emanation of the universe. The urge to give rise to the emergence of the universe should not be seen as a kind of causal necessity existing in the Absolute. It would no more be the Absolute if necessity is imposed upon It. Since the Absolute, according to the Trika, is full and perfect, so no want or lack would be existing in it. As it is the innate nature of the Absolute to emanate as well as to withdraw the emanated, so the question of causal necessity cannot be imposed upon it. If this playful nature is withdrawn from the Absolute, it would be like reducing the absolute powers of the Absolute Godhead to the state of nothingness, which is identical with non-existence. Since such is not the case, the Trika assertion concerning the Absolute as being blissful is thereby logically established. This dramatic playfulness expresses itself perfectly when the Absolute as *aṇu* remains in bondage. Thus bondage and liberation is a dyad that is skillfully played by the Absolute.

The absolutistic theism of Abhinavagupta differs from the one that Śaṁkara enunciated. For Abhinavagupta the essential nature of the Absolute is expressed through two philosophical terms, namely, *prakāśa* and *vimarśa,* which in thelogical terms is equated with *anuttara* and *spanda* respectively. The term *prakāśa* denotes that the Absolute as consciousness is luminous, and on account of this luminosity every existent entity shines forth as manifest category. Were the Absolute to be devoid of the light of consciousness, there would be nothing that could be called manifest, which, in other words, would mean the prevalence of non-existence. In the absence of consciousness as light, there would prevail the darkness of non-existence. The Absolute, however, is not only of the nature of the light of consciousness, but also is endowed with *vimarśa,* which means that it is constantly pulsating. The pulsating nature of consciousness is equated to self-awareness, that is to say, the Absolute is always aware of itself. Had the Absolute been devoid of awareness, it would in no manner be different from a lifeless or inert object. The diamond, for example, contains within itself luminosity, but like an inert object is unaware of itself as being a mass of light. Since the Absolute is identical with *vimarśa,* and thereby with pulsation, it accordingly facilitated the passage for arriving at the conclusion that it is the Absolute itself that is the embodiment of Godhead. Thus such concepts as *vimarśa,* pulsation, energy gave rise to the notion of the Absolute as being Godhead itself. The Absolute as Godhead accordingly engages in the display of the sport of five processes of emanation, preservation of the emanated, dissolution of the emanated, concealment of, and revelation of, the essential nature. This God of Trika is not an entity imposed by an external agency called *māyā.* Rather it is the Absolute itself who, through its own free-will, assumes the role of a theistic God.

Śaṁkara's idea of *brahman* is quite contrary to the one formulated by Abhinavagupta. The *brahman* of Śaṁkara, first and foremost, is *śānta,* which is to say that it is deviod of activity. Although the essential nature of *brahman* is said to be *prakāśa,* yet it is so devoid of pulsation or activity as to be as inert as a stone. This deficiency of activity in *brahman* has been equated to the state of cessation which the Buddhist *nirvāṇa* embodies. It is a state of extinction of everything. On account of this deficiency of awareness in *brahman,* Śaṁkara accordingly has been accused by his critics as being a crypto-Buddhist.

Since such a peaceful *brahman* has no possiblity of being engaged in the manifestation of categories, so an attempt is made to resort to an imaginary God outside *brahman.* This God is propped up by such a kind of *māyā* whose location is unknown and whose existence can neither be affirmed nor denied, because of it being unthinkable. So Advaita Vedānta is unable to explain the existence of the manifest universe. To avoid logical pitfalls, it accordingly maintained that the very existence of the manifest world is as unreal as is that of *māyā.* Also Śaṁkara equated *māyā* to ignorance, and on account of ignorance we identify the real with the unreal, as we do in the case of rope-snake. In the Trika system *māyā* is not illusion, nor is it responsible for propping up an illusory God. Rather *māyā* is the real creative power of God. Although both the systems represent non-dualism as a philosophical interpretation of Reality, yet both of them differ radically from each other in their conception of the Absolute. The Trika of Abhinavagupta represents a philosophical standpoint that is affirmative, whereas the Advaita Vedānta of Śaṁkara embodies a viewpoint that is nagative. One wants to obtain the knowledge of the Absolute through affirmation, whereas the other uses via negativa for the same purpose.

The fault lies in the fact that the followers of Śaṁkara, while adhering to the notion of tranquil *brahman,* do not take into consideration the subtle stir that underlies the Absolute as consciousness. The Trika followers accept the Vedāntic assertion of *brahman* being tranquil, but at the same time it affirms that the peacefulness is not such as would result in the destitution of pulsation of supreme consciousness. The ocean, for example, may be peaceful at the surface level, but underneath the surface lays such pulsation as would result in the emergence of waves. Had the ocean been devoid of pulsation, there would not eventuate the arising of waves. But such is not the case. The waves emerge, and this proves the existence of vibraton underneath the surface of an ocean. This divine pulsation shines forth in the form of blissfulness of the Absolute. This divine blissful stir denotes the power of action (*kriyā-śakti*) of the Godhead, and it is through this power of action that every divine activity of emanation, preservation, dissolution, concealment and revelation is carried out. And it is on account of this power that consciousness is accordingly identified with awareness. It would, therefore, not be wrong to say that the Advaita Vedānta has failed in exploring the interiority of consciousness in the manner the Trika has performed this taks.

Insofar as Buddhists are concerned, they too have failed in looking at consciousness the way the Trika has affirmed its existence. The Therevāda Buddhists are so circumscribed by their empiricism as would not allow them to go beyond their reductionism. They considered consciousness, on the one hand, as being simply a material aggregate (*skanda*) and, on the other hand, considered it to be as fluxional, and thereby inpermanent, as any other insubstantial entity. The doctrine of insubstantiality would not allow them to postulate the existence of a permanent self. Since everything is impermanent, fluxional, and so devoid of a permanent substratum, so the question of permanent self did not oppress their mind at all. For the Theravādins it is becoming that is real, whereas Being is a fiction engendered by imagination.

Insofar as *nirvāṇa* is concerned, it simply embodies the state of extinction. There is, however, a slight improvement with regard to the question of consciousness in the context of Mahāyāna. The Mahāyānists recognised the need for such an entity that could serve the religious needs of the populace. The Yogācāra School recognised the existence of such consciousness that is of the nature of luminosity. They also invented the concept of storehous consciousnes (*ālayavijñāna*), which is seen a kind of a place where all the impressions are deposited.

However, the Yogācārins, in the midst of this improvement, looked at consciousness as being fluxional, and thereby impermanent. Their exploration, thus, stops at the dreamless state, and does not even touch the exterior of the Fourth (*turya*). The Mādhyamika Schools of Nāgārjun established such a doctrine of non-existence as would terminate in the perception of entire objectivity to be identical with the Void (*śūnya*). The objective world is seen to be destitute of an intrinsic nature (*svabhāva*), and so accordingly is identified with nothingness. This extreme nihilism ultimately led to the emergence of Yogācāra, which at least accepts the existence of consciousness, although in a belated manner.

The Vaiṣṇava theism is unable to come out of its mythic mode of understanding, and so has not at all given due consideration to a theism that is absolutistic in its orientation. Insofar as the theism of Nyāya-Vaiśeṣika is concerned, it looks at God in such a manner as would be dependent on so many external elements for carrying out its activities. It is such a God who has hardly any freedom, because its freedom is taken away by being a dependent entity. It is Trika Shaivism alone that seems to have done justice to theistic absolutism by asserthing that the Absolute inheres within itself such Shakti as would terminate in the manifestation of categories without undergoing any kind of transformation or change. In this manner the absoluteness of the Absolute is well maintained. Although transcendent, the Absolute at the same time is immanent, and so accordingly as God is seen as the ultimate source of everything.

1

Salutation To the Deity

परं परस्थं गहनादनादिमेकं निविष्टं बहुधा गुहासु।
सर्वालायं सर्वचराचरस्थं त्वामेव शम्भुं शरणं प्रपद्ये।। १।।

1. Paraṃ parasthaṃ ghanādanādim
Ekaṃ niviṣṭaṃ bahudhā guhāsu
Sarvālayaṃ sarvacarācarasthaṃ
Tvāmeva Śambhuṃ śaraṇaṃ prapadye.

Trs.—Since you, O Śambhū, are transcendentally so situated as to be beyond the reach of mystifying Māyā, so (accordingly) you have, although one, penetrated, in manifold ways, the hearts of all the contingent beings (in such a way) as to be their abode. (Although transcendent, yet) you are immanently present in all the moving and unmoving manifest (categories).

Comment—Although Śambhū may be a transcendent category, which means beyond space and time, yet he is seen to be so immanently present in the phenomena as to be their sole source of existence. In this manner is established the phislsophical principle of non-dualism and in terms of which is explained as to how the manifest categories have been emanated, which is to say that it is Śambhū who has, as it were, vomitted the universe out of himself. It would mean that the manifest categories are the expansion or extension of the own-being of Śambhū. Although having extended himself as the universe, yet it does not taint him in any manner on account of him being beyond the reach of impure category called Māyā. As the transcendent absolute, Śambhū at the same time has Godhead as its essential nature through which the play of emanation and dissolution of phenomena is enacted.

2-3

Introductory Statement

गर्भाधिवासपूर्वकमरणान्तकदुः खचक्रविभ्रान्तः।
आधारं भगवन्तं शिष्यः पप्रच्छ परमार्थम्।। २।।

2. **Garbhādhivāsapūrvaka-**
maraṇāntaka-duḥkha-cakra-vibhrāntaḥ
Ādharaṃ bhagavantaṃ
Śiṣyaḥ papraccha paramārtham.

Trs.—Approaching the Venerable Śeṣa, a disciple, while having (endlessly) traversed the miserable cycle of births/deaths from the time of (conception) in the womb of the mother to the time of death, asks the question as to what constitutes the essence of existence that is absolutely true.

Comment—Ādhāra is another name of Patañjali who is popularly believed to be the incarnation of Śeṣanāga, the serpent god. Śeṣa is supposed to be upholoding the earth underneath.

आधारकारिकाभिस्तं गुरुरभिभाषते स्म तत्सारम्।
कथयत्यभिनवगुप्तः शिवशासनदृष्टियोगेन।। ३।।

3. **Ādhāra-kārikābhistaṃ gurur-**
abhibhāṣatesma tatsāram
Kathayatyabhinavaguptaḥ
Śivaśāsana-dṛṣṭi-yogena.

Trs.—The teacher (who is none other than Patañjali) (engaged in a dialogue in terms of which) a discussion with the disciple on the concerned theme eventuated through the text called *Ādhārakārikā* (which is identical with the *Paramārthasāra* of Patañjali), and (now) the essense of it is being expounded, from the perspective of Shaivism, by Abhinavagupta.

Comment—The original name of the text was *Ādhārakārikā,* and Abhinavagupta made use of it in such a manner as would allow him to extract the essence of the content of the text, which would become a ground for explaining the Shaivite doctrines. Abhinava also made use of the style of the composition of the said text. And the final product that Abhinava produced out of this Vaiṣṇava work is known by the name of *Paramārthasāra.*

4

Four Divisions (*aṇḍas*)

निजशक्तिवैभवभरादण्डचतुष्टयमिदं विभागेन।
शक्तिर्माया **प्रकृतिः** पृथ्वी चेति प्रभावितं प्रभुणा।। ४।।

4. Nijaśakti-vaibhav-bharād-
aṇḍa-catuṣṭayamidaṃ vibhāgena
Śaktirmāyā prakṛtiḥ pṛthvī ceti
prabhāvitaṃ prabhuṇā.

Trs.—The all-powerful Lord, through his (umlimited) glorious divine powers, gave rise to (such) four divisions (of manifestation which are termed) as Śakti, Māyā, Prakṛti and Pṛthvī.

Comment—An *aṇḍa* is such a manifest sphere that contains within itself a number of phenomenal elements whose function it is to conceal the divine nature of the Absolute. The Energy of the Absolute is such a projecting power which allows the emanation of the phenomena to occur, and accordingly is the divinity of the Absolute concealed. Thus the pure unity of the Absolute is disturbed when the first four categories or *tattvas* from Śakti to Vidyā become manifest. The manifest category of Māyā functions in such a manner as would push into oblivion the pure unity and potency of the Absolute by allowing the five sheaths or *kañcukas* to emerge, which would lead to the emergence of a contracted being called Puruṣa. The sphere of Māyā consists of seven *tattvas* from Māyā to Puruṣa. Insofar as the sphere of Prakṛti is concerned, it contains within itself the category of Puruṣa along with the sense organs, *tanmātras,* the *guṇas* and the four gross elements upto water. This sphere contains within itself twenty-three *tattvas,* which is to say from Prakṛti to Water. Lastly, we have the sphere of Pṛthvī. This category embodies solidity, and so accordingly is completely gross. It represents the universe as being completely gross. Apart from these spheres, there is Śiva-*tattva,* which transends all these categories.

5

The Enjoyer

तत्रान्तर्विश्वमिदं विचित्रतनुकरणभुवनसन्तानम्।
भोक्ता च तत्र देही शिव एव गृहीतपशुभावः।। ५।।

5. Tatrāntarviśvamidaṃ
vicitra-tanukaraṇa-bhuvana-santānaṃ
Bhoktā ca tatra dehī
Śiva eva gṛhita-paśu-bhvāḥ.

Trs.—The entire universe together with its wonderfully (crafted)variety of bodies, sense organs and a series of worlds are to be found (existing) within the (confines) of these four spheres. The (ever changing) contingent being, as the experiencer of pleasure and pain, also exists there. (This limited individual being) is none other than Śiva himself, who (out of its own free will) has become the bound contingent embodied being.

Comment—In this verse the basic doctrine of Trika is explained in terms of the *a priori* assertion that the universe, including the limited contingent beings, is but the self-extension or expansion of the Absolute, who is but a mass of bliss and consciousness. It is the inherent nature of the Absolute to play the game of vomitting the universe out of itself as well as resorbing the emanated. There, thus, exists fundamental identity between the Absolute and the universe, because the latter is the grossification of the former. Thus it is Śiva himself who, like an animal, is fettered by the ropes of karman, and so accordingly undergoes the cycle of rebirths till the time liberation from bondage is realized.

6-7

One Manifesting itself as Many

नानाविधवर्णानां रूपं धत्ते यथाऽमलः स्फटिकः।
सुरमानुषपशुपादपरूपत्वं तद्वदीशोऽपि।। ६।।

6. Nānā-vidha-varṇānāṃ rūpaṃ
dhatte yathāmalaḥ sphaṭikaḥ
Sura-mānuṣa-paśu-pādapa-
rūpatvaṃ tadvadīśo' pi.

Trs.—As the immaculate crystal has (the capacity of apprehending) the variegated appearances of various hues and colours which are reflected in it, likewise does the absolute Lord (out of its own free will) project himself as a deity, a human being, an animal, and a plant (by reflecting them in his own mirror).

Comment—This verse delineates the idea of the process of manifestation of the categories from Sadāśiva to the Earth. While reflecting in the mirror of consciousness the entire objectivity, there does not occur any kind of taint in the essential being of the Lord. This is analogous to the reflection of objects in the physical mirror. While objects are being reflected in the mirror, the purity of the mirror in no manner is affected. The other analogy is that of crystal. A crystal, while apprehending a variety of colours, does not undergo any kind of change. The Lord, while unfolding the process of manifestation of categories, does it independently, which is to say out of its own free will. The Lord has no need of any external substance. Also the doctrine of causal transformation (*pariṇāmavāda*) is not applicable to the Lord. The fundamental cause for the manifestation of objectivity is his playfulness. Thus the Vedāntic doctrine of *avidyā/māyā* as being the cause of manifestation is done away with. Likewise is negated the Yogācāra doctrine of *vāsanās* being the cause of the universe. In the Trika system of thought it is the playful nature of the Lord which is the cause of the manifestation of phenomena.

गच्छति गच्छति जल इव हिमकरबिम्बं स्थिते स्थितिं याति।
तनुकरणभुवनवर्गे तथाऽयमात्मा महेशानः।। ७।।

7. Gacchati gacchati jala iva
himakara-bimbaṃ sthite sthitiṃ yāti
Tanu-karaṇa-bhuvana-varge
tathāyamātmā maheśānaḥ.

Trs.—As the reflected disc of the moon in the flowing waters (of a stream) appears to be moving (along with the flowing waters) and (likewise) appears to be unmoving in waters that are stationary, so does this expansive *ātman* manifest itself in diverse ways in the form of such categories as bodies, sense organs and the worlds.

Comment—This verse explains as to what constitutes the nature of dependence and independence. The moon is such an entity that embodies within itself such characteristics which denote dependence. It is so dependent on elements other than itself as would enable it to be reflected in the moving or static waters. It has to borrow the light from the sun so that its reflection could be reflected in the waters of a pool or stream. Likewise it reflects itself in that which is other than itself. In the case of *ātman* such dependence is not applicable. *Ātman* is completely independent. Whatever it does, it does in accordance with its own free will. While reflecting the categories (*tattvas*) outwardly, *ātman* reflects them in its own mirror, which is to say that the reflection occurs in the mirror of Consciousness, which is the nature of *ātman*. Also appearance of entities is not necessitated by chance; rather it is the playful nature of the *ātman* to manifest what is inside it.

8

The Appearance of Consciousness

राहुरदृश्योऽपि यथा शशिबिम्बस्थ: प्रकाशते तद्वत्।
सर्वगतोऽप्ययमात्मा विषयाश्रयणेन धीमुकुरे।। ८।।

8. Rāhuradṛśyo'pi yathā
śaśi-bimbasthaḥ prakāśate tadvad
Sarva-gato'pyayamātmā
viṣayāsrayaṇena dhīmukure.

Trs.—*Ātman,* while shining in the mirror of its own intelligence, witnesses (the entirety) of objective reflection (out there) in the same manner as does occur the appearance of invisible Rāhu in the disc of the moon

Comment—It is believed by the Indian astrologers that Rāhu is always on the move in the sky. He, however, disappears, or should we say, becomes invisible, as and when he directs his attention towards the moon. This analogy is used to explain as to how the *ātman,* though infinite and all-pervading, appears as the "I" only if it reflects itself in the mirror of its own intelligence, which means that as an embodied "I" the *ātman* at the mental level has such experiences which objectivity generates. Thus the *ātman* as a contracted or limited individual expresses the experiences that accrue to it in terms of "I saw that beautiful object yesterday." Such an appearance of the *ātman* as an "I" occurs only in a conscious individual being and not in objects that are inert.

9

The Appearance of the Divine

आदर्शे मलरहिते यद्वद्वदनं विभाति तद्वदयम्।
शिवशक्तिपातविमले धीतत्त्वे भाति भारूपः।। ९।।

9. Ādarśe mala-rahite yadvad
vadanaṃ vibhāti tadvadayaṃ
Śiva-śaktipāta-vimale
dhī-tattve bhāti bhārūpaḥ.

Trs.—The (lustrous nature) of *ātman*, in the form of immaculate consciousness, shines in the intelligence that is (perfectly) purified by the grace of Śiva in the same manner as the appearance of one's face eventuates in a mirror that is free from (the dust) of taints.

Comment—Trika Shaivism of Kashmir is characterised by the mysticism of grace (*saktipāta*). Doctrinally it is asserted that apart from the divine grace of Shiva, nothing much spiritually can be achieved. Grace is viewed as being such a power which provides the necessary impetus for the success of any undertaking. Thus grace is seen as being responsible in generating the necessary inclination in an individual towards that which has a divine orientation. It is through grace that there occurs appropirate contact between the aspirant and his teacher, which accordingly terminates in the inward purification. Being pure inwardly, the aspirant has the illuminative realisation of identity with the Absolute.

10-11

The Absolute as Paramaśiva

भारूपं परिपूर्णं स्वात्मनि विश्रान्तितो महानन्दम्।
इच्छासंवित्करणैर्निर्भरितमनन्तशक्तिपरिपूर्णम्।। १०।।

सर्वविकल्पविहीनं शुद्धं शान्तं लयोदयविहीनम्।
यत्परतत्त्वं तस्मिन्विभाति षट्त्रिंशदात्मजगत्।। ११।।

10. Bhārūpaṃ paripūraṇaṃ
svātmani viśrāntito mahānandam
Ichhā-saṁvit-karaṇair
nirbharitamananta-śakti-paripūrṇaṃ.

11. Sarva-vikalpa-vihīnam
śuddhaṃ śāntam layodaya-vihīnam
yat paratattvaṃ tasmin vibhāti
ṣaṭtrimśadātma jagat.

Trs.—The entire (emanated) objectivity, which consists of thirty-six categories, (not only become) manifest (but also) shine forth in the Absolute who (essentially) shines as the light of pure consciousness (and accordingly is termed as being) perfect in evry respect, full of infinite blisss on account of being (fully) independent, while (at the same time) reposing in itself. (This Absolute) also comprises of such functions as willing, knowing and doing (which means that) it is full of divine powers, is totally devoid of thought-constructs. (Above all, the Absolute) is (as) pure and tranquil within itself as to be totally free from the process of dissolution and emergence.

Comment—The Trika system of thought adheres to the notion that the Absolute always shines forth on account of it being of the nature of light. The basic nature of the Absolute as consciousness is, thus, to be luminous, which means that all the thirty-six categories, prior to their manifestation, shine forth within the Absolute. It would mean that the Absolute contains within itself the entire phenomena prior to their manifestation. When manifested, these categories appear as manifest categories due to the light of consciousness. This assertion would mean that nothing exists apart from consciousness. Whatever there is in the world, including the world itself, owes its existence to consciousness. It is the Free Will of the Absolute that allows the emergence of the categories to occur. The Absolute as Godhead is endowed with such three powers—will, knowledge and action—through which all the divine activities are conducted. When we speak of the Absolute as consciousness, it means that it is tranquil, beyond time and space, eternal, devoid of thought-constructs. As I-consciousness, the Absolute is both light and reflective awareness, which is to say that it is both *prakāśa* and *vimarśa.* It is at this point where the Trika differs radically from Vedānta concerning the nature of the Absolute. In the Vedāntic system of thought the Absolute is seen simply as *prakāśa,* which would mean that it is not the Absolute who brings about the manifestation of the universe. Instead of *brahman,* it is *avidyā* which is seen as the source of an unreal world. In the Trika it is not *avidyā* which is the source of an unreal world; rather it is Shiva who himself gives rise to the emergence of the world that is real. Thus the world that appears as a manifest category owes its existence to the light of consciousness. Accordingly is Absolute spoken of as being a mass of consciousness and bliss.

12-13

The Theory of Rflection and the Appearance of Diversity

दर्पणबिम्बे यद्वन्नगरग्रामादि चित्रमविभागि।
भाति विभागेनैव च परस्परं दर्पणादपि च।। १२।।
विमलतमपरमभैरवबोधात्तद्वद्विभागशून्यमपि।
अन्योन्यं च ततोऽपि च विभक्तमाभाति जगदेतत्।। १३।।

12. Darpaṇa-bimbe yadvan
nagara-grāmādi citramavibhāgi
Bhāti vibāgenaiva ca
parasparaṃ darpaṇādapi ca.

13. Vimalatama-parama-bhairava-
bodhāt tadvad vibhāga-śūnyamapi
Anyonyaṃ ca tato'pi ca
vibhaktamābhāti jagadetat.

Trs.—As the reflections of some multi-variety object like a town, a village, and so on appear or shine within a mirror in such a manner as if they (viz. the reflections), though not different from the mirror, appear to be separate from it, likewise do all the phenomenal (entities) appear to be different not only mutually (from each other), but also from the absolute Consciousness (which is said to be) infinite, pure, divine and perfect (in all its essentials) (and accordingly is) called Bhairava (denoting thereby) Almighty God. (All these entities, in fact), are not different from the Absolute.

Comment—It is assumed by the Trika thinkers that the theory of reflection explains in a much better way than any other theory that no change or transformation occurs in the absolute I-consiousness in the precess of manifestation of categories from Sadāśiva down to Earth. The Trika doctrine maintains that what is emitted as the phenomenl categories is nothing else than what lies potentially within the Absolute itself. This idea is explained by resorting to the analogy of peacock and its colourful plumage. The phenomenal entities, prior to their manifestation, exist in the Absolute in the same manner as does the colourful plumage of a peacock exist in the juice of an egg. This analogy could further be delineated by resorting to the image of a seed and plant. The crux of the theory, on the one hand, is that every phenomenl category shines in the Absolute in the same manner as a reflection appears in a mirror and, on the other hand, it explains that no taint or deficiency occurs in the nature of the Absolute when engaged in giving rise to manifestation. Also it explains that there occurs the perception of difference between the mirror and the reflection, although the reflection may not be different from the mirror. Thus the theory implies that every phenomenal category shines in the Absolute in the same manner as a reflection appears in a mirror. There is, however, such a difference between consciousness and a mirror which points out the contingent nature of the latter. The mirror is a contingent entity because it needs such a help of external instrumentalities as would facilitate the occurring of reflection in it. In the case of consciousness such a rule is inapplicable, as I-consciousness reflects everything in its own mirror due to its divinity. The I-consciousness does not need to resort to *avidyā* of Vedānta or to the Buddhist *vāsanās* for the purpose of manifesting categories. There is another difference that distinguishes I-consciousness from the mirror. The mirror is an inert object, whereas the mirror of I-consciounsess is permeated by *vimarśa*. The mirror is an inert object and so has no awareness of itself or of reflections that are reflected in it, whereas consciousness is aware of itself as well as of reflections that shine in its own mirror. Thus the Trika is not afraid, as is Advaita Vedānta, of ascribing activity to the Absolute. The Absolute of Trika consists of both *prakāśa* and *vimarśa.*

14

The Pure Emanation

शिवशक्तिसदाशिवतामीश्वरविद्यामयीं च तत्त्वदशाम्।
शक्तीनां पञ्चानां विभक्तभावेन भासयति।। १४।।

14. Śiva-śakti-sadāśivatāṃ
īśvara-vidyā-mayīm ca tattva-daśām
Saktīnām pañcānāṃ
vibhakta-bhāvena bhāsayati.

Trs.—The manifestation of the states of the five pure categories of Śiva, Śakti, Sadāśiva, Īśvara and Vidyā are brought about by the Absolute through the outward projection of the five main powers of (*cit, ānanda, icchā, jñāna* and *kriyā*). (These five divine powers constitute the essential nature of the Absolute).

Comment—The Trika idea of the Absolute is redically different from the one propounded by Śaṁkara. The Absolute of Śaṁkara is so tranquil, like an inanimate object, as to be devoid of self-awareness. It is for this reason that he was called a crypto Buddhist. In contrast to the tranquil *brahman* of Śaṁkara, the Trika adheres to such a notion of the Absolute as would be perfectly endowed with divine powers. The basic divine powers of the Absolute are said to be five, namely, consciousness, bliss, will, knowledge and action. All these powers function through mutual cooperation, yet each of them is, at the same time, independent. Each power is predominant only in one category.

The power of consciousness is said to be dominant in the category of Paramaśiva, and as such projects itself in the form of the category of Śiva. It is in the category of Śiva in which the power of blissfulness is predominant. When blissfulness projects itself, it shines in the category of Śakti in the form of the power of will. It is in the category of Sadāśiva in which emerges the power of will with the predominance of knowledge. Accordingly emerges the category of Īśvara, which is dominated by the power of action. It is action that gives rise to Vidyā category. It is a category that adheres to knowledge that is error free, and accordingly the place of prominance is given to knowledge.

With regard to the predominance of powers in the categories, each power is predominant in a particular category in accordance with the nature of the category as well as of the power. In the *Śivadṛṣṭi* of Somānanda and the *Īśvarapratyabhijñā* of Utpalācārya the correspondence of powers to their respective categories is so structured as to begin from Paramaśiva down to Īśvara. In the *Tantrāloka* of Abhinavagupta the correlation of powers is from the category of Śiva to that of Vidyā category.

The highest category is that of Paramaśiva—a category that is viewed as being of the nature of infinite consciousness. Insofar as the category of Śiva is concerned, it is another name for the Absolute, which as pure consciousness embodies noumenal aspect of reality. It is Śiva who is considered to be the ultimate source of the manifestation of phenomenal categories, whereas the category of Śakti provides the necessary impetus to Śiva for actualising the process of manifestation. In these two categories of Śiva and Śakti, however, no objective manifestation occurs because in them it is I-consciousness that alone shines, whereas this-ness is completely absent. These two categories offer perfect non-dual unity, and the aspirant who realises this state of unity is callled Akula.

15

The Impure Emanation

परमं यत्स्वातन्त्र्यं दुर्घटसम्पादनं महेशस्य।
देवी मायाशक्तिः स्वात्मावरणं शिवस्यैतत्।। १५।।

**15. Paramaṃ yat svātantryaṃ
durghaṭa-sampādanaṃ maheśasya
Devī māyā-śaktiḥ
svātmāvaranaṃ Śivasyaitat.**

Trs.—It is the divine power (or deity), called *māyā-śakti,* through which the absolutely Free Paramaśiva brings into being that which (seemingly) may be impossible (to the worldly people). It is this (deified power which enables) Paramaśiva to veil himself (in such a manner as to conceal his essential nature).

Comment—The Trika concept of *māyā* is not the same as is found in the philosophy of Śaṁkara. For Śaṁkara it is such a negative entity whose abode is unknown. It is and it is not. It is there to the extent illusion exists. Upon the negation of illusion, *māyā* disappears. We can neither affirm it nor deny it, and that is why it is spoken of as being unthinkable. The Trika, in contrast to the Advaita Vedānta, has a positive understanding of *māyā.* It is seen such a power of the Lord which, when projected outwardly, manifests itself as the sixth category termed as Māyā on the scale of divine descent. It is on account of the power of *māyā* that the Absolute so covers himself as to become, as it were, *Deus absconditus* or should we say, God of absence. Assuming the limitations of an individual, the Lord thereby experiences everything in terms of diversity, which means forgetfulness of one's divine nature. It is from the category of Māyā from which proceed all such elements that are inert. This category may be seen serving as the substratum of numerous floating universes like the bubbles in an ocean. The category belongs to the realm of the impure path *(aśuddhādhvan)*. When categories emanate from the category of Māyā, their emanation is conducted under the supervision of Anantanātha.

16-17

Manifestation of Sheaths (*kañcukas*)

मायापरिग्रहवशाद्बोधो मलिनः पुमान्पशुर्भवति।
कालकलानियतिवशद्रागाविद्यावशेन सम्बद्धः।। १६।।

16. Māyā-parigraha-vaśād
bodho malinaḥ pumān paśur bhavati
Kāla-kalā-niyati-vaśād
rāgāvidyā-vaśena saṃbaddhaḥ.

Trs.—The absolute I-consciousness, upon making *māyā* as a (necessary) part of itself, assumes impurity (in such a manner) as to become a finite (and limited) being called *puruṣa.* (Upon becoming a *puruṣa,* the Absolute appears) like a bound animal (who is fettered by the ropes of such bondage) which consist of *kāla, kalā, niyati, rāga* and *avidyā* corresponding respectively to temporality, to the performance of such actions that are limited, to causality that is determinate, to an attachment that is limited to temporal objects, and to knowledge that has the capacity to know a little.

Comment—The Trika concept of *puruṣa* is quite different from the self-monad of Sāṁkhya. The *puruṣa* of Sāṁkhya, though passive, exists eternally in opposition to equally eternal *prakṛti.* This passive *puruṣa* somehow gets entangled with *prakṛti* and accordingly becomes a bound being. The *puruṣa* of Trika emerges when the Absolute so contracts himself as to become an individual being or *aṇu* who has limited knowledge and can only perform limited deeds. This contracted individual experiences everything as being different from himself. Thus it is the impurity of limitedness and of difference that are constitutive of the finite I-consciousness of the limited individual being. He is so veiled by ignorance as to be chained by the fetters of bondage, and accordingly is equated to an animal that is tied to the peg by the ropes of bondage.

The emergence of phenomenality is further facilitated by Anantanātha when he churns the category of Māyā, and thereby is accordingly facilitated the emergence of five coverings or *kañcukas.* The function of these sheaths is to veil the essential nature of the *ātman,* and in doing so the *ātman* is thereby reduced to the state of a bound *paśu* or animal. Shorn off of its divinity by the *kañcukas,* the *ātman* is so made to function by *kalā* as to have limited capacity to perform deeds. Likewise is the omniscience of the *ātman* so contracted as to give rise to knowledge that is impure, which means the emergence of knowledge that is erroneous. The *ātman* is further contracted when it is made to function under the thumb of *niyati,* or what may be called the determinate causality. This determinate causality restricts the individual in the field of knowledge, action as well as attachment. Finally, temporality is so imposed upon the *ātman* as to make it a finite creature. It is the finitude of time that really expresses as to what limitation with regard to knowledge and action mean. This Trika view of time delineats the idea that time is a construct of the mind, and accordingly actions and events in space are measured in terms of succession. This view of time emerges on account of the individual existing at the level of Māyā. The finite I-consciousness is termed as *puruṣa* when veiled by the five *kañcukas.* As a result of these *kañcukas,* the *ātman* is reduced to the state of bondage.

अधुनैव किंचिदेवेदमेव सर्वात्मनैव जानामि।
मायासहितं कञ्चुकषट्कमणोरन्तरङ्गमिदमुक्तम्।। १७।।

17. Adhunaiva kiñcidevedameva sarvātmanaiva jānāmi Māyā-sahitaṃ kañcuka-ṣaṭkamaṇorantaraṅgamidamuktam.

Trs.—Whatever I know "I know only now and know it only little," which means that "this much I know quite completely." (This kind of knowing is the result of) a group of six sheaths together with Māyā. (These six sheaths are understood) as being the interior limitations of the contracted individual.

Comment—The process of descent of Paramaśiva towards the manifestation of phenomenal categories from *puruṣa* to Earth is characterised by such a form of contraction (*saṁkoca*) as is delineated by the five veils (*kañcukas*). The sheath of *kalā* is responsible in reducing the transcendent Absolute to the level of a finite individual who is so circumscribed by limitations as to be called *aṇu*. The expansiveness of the Absolute gets lost in the oblivion of limitations. Likewise the omniscience of the Absolute, through the sheath of impure *vidyā,* is transformed into such forms of knowledge as would lend itself to error, which is to say, to ignorance. Keeping this context in view, the *Śivasūtras* spoke of all the modes of empirical knowledge as the source of bondage. Accordingly the Fullness of Paramaśiva is formalised in the limited individual as a kind of incompleteness. The incompleteness, thus, expresses itself through the category of attachment (*rāga*). The limited individual seeks association of things in order to overcome the vacuum of finitude within himself. Insofar as the Absolute as eternal is concerned, it is so corroded as to be subservient to time (*kāla*) and to determinate causality (*niyati*). Thus the absolute Freedom (*svātantrya*) loses its lustre when Paramaśiva becomes a bound being.

The initial process of descent to manifestiation is eventuated in and through the five categories from Śiva to Śuddhavidyā, and these categories are accordingly termed as pure path (*śuddhādhvan*) After the emanation of pure categories, there occurs the manifestation of impure elements (*aśuddhādhvan*), which consists of six sheaths and *purusa,* totalling the number of manifest categories as being twelve. These six sheaths are seen as representing the internal limitations of the individual. These limitations, as it were, constitute the nature of an individual being. A *puruṣa* has become an individual being precisely because of *kañcukas.* Had he been deviod of limitations, he would have been abiding either in the plane of pure Vidyā or Shakti.

18

Discarding of Sheaths

कम्बुकमिव तण्डुलकणविनिविष्टं भिन्नमप्यभिदा।
भजते तत्तु विशुद्धिं शिवमार्गौन्मुख्ययोगेन।। १८।।

18. Kumbukamiva taṇḍulakaṇa-
vinivisṭaṃ bhinnamapyabhidā
Bhajate tattu viśuddhiṃ
Śiva-margaunmukya-yogena

Trs.—The *puruṣa,* though different from the *kañcukas,* appears to be so intimate as to be non-different from them like the yellowish covering of the grains of rice, which, however, can (easily) be removed (by cultivating) the contemplative practice of Shaiva yoga.

Comment—The analogy of the husk of rice grain is so made use of as to explain it in terms of the limitedness of the individual existent. Insofar as the grain of rice is covered by the husk, to that extent the real nature of rice will never be known. It is upon the removal of the outer husk and the inner yellowish covering that we come to know the real nature of rice, which shines forth in the form of white glow. Similarly Śiva is made to experience the finitude of individuality when the five sheaths so cover his essential nature as to suffer from the contraction of knowledge and action. Also the sheaths of determinate causality and time corrode the absolute Freedom by making the individual being the creature of temporality, thereby replacing eternity with temporality. All the sheaths collectively as well as individually function in a manner as to make Śiva such a limited being as to be in bondage. The situation, however, is not so damaging as to be beyond any kind of remedy. The Trika Shaivism has discovered such means or *upāyas* as would render the functioning of sheaths impotent. If the prescribed spiritual path of Trika is cultivated with devotion, the removal of the sheaths, like the husk of the grain of rice, accordingly would result in the restoration of one's essential nature in terms of the realisation of being non-different from the Absolute.

19-20

The Senses and the Organs

सुखदु:खमोहमात्रं निश्चयसंकल्पनाभिमानाच्च।
प्रकृतिरथान्त:करणं बुद्धिमनोऽहङ्कृति क्रमश:॥ १९॥

19. Sukha-duḥkha-moha-mātraṃ
niścaya-saṅkalpanābhimānācca
Prakṛtirathāntaḥkaraṇaṃ
buddhimano'haṅkṛti kramaśaḥ.

Trs.—*Prakrti* is understood as being a collection of (such experiences as, for example), pleasure, pain and delusion (which is to say of ignorance). There are also three interior instrumentalities of (1) *buddhi,* the faculty of understanding, (ii) *manas* or the mind which is seen as being responsible in facilitating the rise of thought-constructs, and (iii) *ahaṅkāra,* the psycho-physical construct called ego.

Comment—*Prakṛti* or what may be called material Nature provides sufficient ingredients to the contracted individual (*aṇu*) in terms of which he has such experiences as are characterized by pleasure, pain and delusional ignorance. The content of such experiences usually corresponds to the constitutents (*guṇas)* of material Nature known as goodness (*sattva*), passion (*rajas*) and darkness (*tamas*). When these constituents are in the state of equilibrium, or should we say devoid of any conflict, there occurs no such activity or undertaking as would terminate in the emergence of phenomenal categories. In the Sāṁkhya system both *prakṛti* and *puruṣa* are such polarities in which the former is seen as being active and the latter as passive. The passive *puruṣa* somehow gets entangled with *prakṛti,* and accordingly is caught up in the web of bondage. The only way *puruṣa* would obtain freedom from this bondage is by gaining the power of discrimination (*viveka*), which is to say by differentiating matter from spirit. However, in the Trika system both *puruṣa* and *prakṛti* are not self-existing eternal categories. They, rather, owe their existence to the Blessed Anantanātha. Īśvara assumes the from of Śrīkaṇṭhanātha upon descending to the level of three constituents of *prakṛti.* When Śrīkaṇṭhanātha disturbs *prakṛti* as well as the equiliburium of the three constituents, there is initiated the emergence of objectivity through the process of transformation. The process of transformation results initially in the emergence of the interior senses of ego, mind and intellect and lastly, there is the manifestation of the gross physical elements known as the *bhūtas.* In the Sāṁkhya the process of transformation is initiated by *prakṛti* itself. This view of self-causation of the Sāṁkhya with regard to *prakṛti* is rejected by the Trika. The Trika, thus, maintains that it is Śrīkaṇṭhanātha who initiates the process of transformation within *prakṛti* by disturbing it as well as its constituents. This transformation of *prakṛti* results in the coming into being of twenty-three categories from the *mahat-tattva* to Earth. As *prakṛti* is considered to be inert, so it is devoid of such capacity as would enable it to transform itself into various categories. It is for this reason that Śrīkaṇṭhanātha as the causal agent for initiating the process of transformation has been postulated.

श्रोत्रं त्वगक्षि रसना घ्राणं बुद्धीन्द्रियाणि शब्दादौ।
वाक्पाणिपादपायूपस्थं कर्मेन्द्रियाणि पुनः।। २०।।

20. Śrotram tvagakṣi-rasanā-ghrānaṃ
buddhīndriyanī śabdādau
Vāk-pāṇi-pāda-payūpasthaṃ
karmendriyāni punaḥ.

Trs.—(Insofar as) the external senses are (concerned), they are quite helpful in grasping (such) objects as sound, touch, smell, etc. Thus the *śrotra* is the auditory sense, *tvac* represents the sense of touch, *akṣi* embodies the sense of sight, *rasanā* is the sense (through which we have the experience) of taste, and it is the sense of *ghṛana* through which we smell things. Likewise the external senses help us to engage in activities that are external. Thus through the organ of speech—*vāc*—we speak, through the organ of *pāṇi* we grasp things, through the organ called *pāda* we move about, through the organ of *payū* we discharge waste, and through the organ of *upastha* we experience sexual delight.

Comment—The basic function of the senses is cognitive in the sense of enabling the individual to appropriate and assimilate such experiences that would give rise to knowldge. The eyes, for example, allow the individual to have the perception of objects that translates into knowledge when conceptualisation occurs of what has been perceived. Mere perception of an object must not be equated with knowledge. An animal also perceives things out there, but he has no knowledge of them. Thus all the senses have corresponding objects of perception. When different perceptions of different senses are collected together, we have knowledge that is wholesome. Insofar as the organs of actions are concerned, they function mechanically and are not in any manner the source of knowledge. These organs have the possibility of functioning in a dual way. For example, it is through mouth that we speak as well as eat food. Mouth can also grasp things with the help of teeth. Tongue has the power of tasting things as well as uttering a speech. All these senses as well as organs are the result of the transformation of *prakṛti* initiated by Śrīkaṇṭhanātha.

21-22

The Subtle and Gross Elements

एषां ग्राह्यो विषयः सूक्ष्मः प्रविभागवर्जितो यः स्यात्।
तन्मात्रपञ्चकं तच्छब्दः स्पर्शो महो रसो गन्धः।। २१।।

21. Eṣāṃ grāhyo viśayaḥ sūkṣmaḥ
pravibhāga-varjito yaḥ syāt
Tanmātra-pañcakaṃ tat śabdaḥ
sparśo maho raso gandhaḥ.

Trs.—The five subtle and undifferentiated objects that have to be apprehended by the (corresponding) senses are the sound, touch, light, taste and smell respectively. These are termed (collectively) as the *tanmātras.*

Comment—*Tantmātra,* which means simply "that much," is to be viewed as the subtle form of an object devoid of special or particular characteristics. Thus all such objects as sound, light, touch, taste and smell are free from the weight of form, colour, size, etc. What it entails is the suchness of th object that is denoted by the term *tanmātra.* These objects, called *tanmātras,* are the result of the transformation of ego. All these objects are apprehended by the senses in terms of feelings and ideas that are closely associated with the ego. It is natural for the ego to assimilate these objects as particulars, and accordingly appear itself in and through them.

एतत्संसर्गवशात्स्थूलो विषयस्तु भूतपञ्चकताम्।
अभ्येति नभः पवनस्तेजः सलिलं च पृथ्वी च।। २२।।

22. Etat-saṃsarga-vaśāt sthūlo
viṣayastu bhūta-pañcakatām
Abhyeti nabhaḥ pavanas-tejaḥ
salilaṃ ca pṛthvī ca.

Trs.—It is through the process of churning up of subtle objects that there appears objective form of existence in terms of the five gross physical elements known as the *pañca-bhūtas,* namely, ether, air, fire, water and earth

Comment—It is through the process of mixing and disturbing the subtle sense objects that there emerge accordingly the corresponding gross categories of existence. The gross objects, upon their appearance, carry with themselves the special characteristics (*viśeṣa-guṇa*) of subtle objects. The formation of the gross objects may be seen as the congealing of the subtle objects.

23-24

Three Veils of Consciousness

तुष इव तण्डुलकणिकामावृणुते प्रकृतिपूर्वकः सर्गः।
पृथ्वीपर्यन्तोऽयं चैतन्यं देहभावेन।। २३।।

23. Tuṣa iva taṇḍula-kaṇikāmāvṛṇute
prakṛti-pūrvakaḥ sargaḥ
Pṛthvī-paryanto'yaṃ
caitanyaṃ dehabhāvena.

Trs.—The emergence of all the elements from *prakṛti* to Earth, like the husk-coverd grain of rice, manifest themselves either (in the form) of gross or subtle elements of the individualised consciousness, (and accordingly function) as coverings (and thereby) conceal (the essential nature of consciousness).

Comment—Whether the elements are gross or subtle, they come into being only when there occurs mixing up of elements by causing disturbance in the equilibrium of the constitutents of *prakṛti.* Upon the emergence of the elements, they become an inseperable part of the individualised consciousness, and accordingly the finite consciousness identifies itself with them in such a manner as if they embody the self. Insofar as the *kañcukas* are concerned, they constitute the interior limitations of the finite self, and thereby cause the concealment of the essential nature of consciousness.

परमावरणं मल इह सूक्ष्मं मायादि कञ्चुकं स्थूलम्।
बाह्यं विग्रहरूपं कोशत्रयवेष्टितो ह्यात्मा।। २४।।

24. Paramāvaraṇam mala iha sūkṣmaṃ
māyādi-kañcukaṃ sthūlaṃ
Bāhyaṃ vigraha-rūpaṃ
kośa-traya-veṣṭito hyātmā.

Trs.—*Mala* is (considered) as being the fundamental impurity and as such (constitutes) the finer covering of consciousness. (Insofar as) the six *kañcukas* from *māyā* to *niyati* are concerned, they (represent) the subtle aspects of the process of veiling, whereas the body (is said to be embodying) the gross aspect. Thus the Self is covered by these Veils.

Comment—The Trika doctrine of manifestation of categories maintains that the Absolute, while descending from universality to particularity, so contracts its universality, through the process of concealment of the essential nature, as to assume the form of a limited individual. In other words, Śiva as a contracted individual becomes so ignorant of himslf as to be deviod of knowledge with regard to his essential nature, which is characterised by divinity, ominiscience, omnipotence and infinitude. Such a state of affairs occurs because of three impurities as well as due to the veiling function of *kañcukas.* The three impurties are the *āṇava-mala, māyīya-mala* and *kārma-mala.* The *āṇava-mala* gives rise to the feeling of being limited, whereas *māyīya-mala* terminates in the rise of such cognitions as are of the nature of difference. The *kārma-mala* leads to the performance of such deeds that actualise the wheel of rebirth. Insofar as the *kañcukas* are concerned, they proceed from the womb of *māyā,* and accordingly function as the interior limitations of the individual. The external limitations of an individual are represented by the gross body. The essential nature of the *ātman,* in such a situation, remains concealed. This very concealment of the essential nature is called ignorance or *avidyā.* It is upon the removal of coverings and of impurities that the real nature of the *ātman* is revealed.

25

Ignorance based View

अज्ञानतिमिरयोगादेकमपि स्वं स्वभावमात्मानम्।
ग्राह्यग्राहकनानावैचित्र्येणावबुध्येत।। २५।।

25. Ajñāna-timara-yogād-ekamapi svaṃ svabhāvamātmānam Grāhya-grāhaka-nānā-vaicitryenāvabuddhyeta.

Trs.—(One of the characteristic feature of) the individualised consciousness is that it suffers from such an eye-disease as darkness (ignorance). (As a consequence of such a disease) the limited individual perceives himself (as being diversified) into multitude of subjects and objects while (in fact) he is nothing else than one non-dual consciousness.

Comment—Ignorance in the Trika system of thought does not denote the absence of knowledge. If ignorance is considered as being equal to the absence of knowledge, then there would be no possibility for knowledge to arise. Since knowledge arises, so it would mean that ignorance is nothing else than incomplete knowledge (*apūrṇa khyāti*). While comparing ignorance to the faulty vision of the eye, Trika thereby offers a rational argument for the emergence of complete knowledge (*pūrṇa-khyāti*). It is upon the rectification of the disease in the eye that the perfect vision is restored. As the jaundiced man, for example, sees everything as being yellowish, likewise does a man of ignorance perceive the one non-dual Absolute as being constituted by diversity. As a result of this faulty perception, an ignorant person goes on committing such deeds the fruits of which he has to reap during the course of his transmigratory existence. It is upon the cognition of unity with the Absolute that the complexity of transmigration comes to an end, and thereby also comes to an end the dual form of experience of pain and pleasure.

26

The Appearance of the Many

रसफाणितशर्करिकागुडखण्डाद्या यथेक्षुरस एव।
तद्वदवस्थाभेदाः सर्वे परमात्मनः शम्भोः।। २६।।

26. Rasa-phāṇita-śarkarikā-guḍa-khaṇḍādyā yathekṣu-rasa eva Tad-vadavasthā-bhedaḥ sarve paramātmanaḥ Śambhoḥ.

Trs.—As the appearance of (diversified) phenomena (have to be seen) as the manifestation of different states of one Universal Śiva, so is the (appearance) of the refined juice, gross juice, grossest juice (called molasses) and the refiend sugar (to be viewed) as the manifestation of a (single) juice of sugarcane.

Comment—The Divine appearance, according to the Trika thought, occurs either in noumenal or phenomenal forms, which is to say that the Absolute expresses itself as being either transcendent or immanent. When viewed from the transcendent perspective, the Absolute is awesome on account of it being infinite, and so beyond the reach of human thinking. This transcendent Absolute, at the same time, is possessed of such divine powers which constitute his Godhead. It is through these divine powers that the Absolute manifests itself in diversified phenomena, and accordingly is made to shine forth in the form of reflection in a mirror—the mirror being the

Absolute itself. What it means is this, the phenomenal diversity appears as reflections in the mirror of divine Consciousness. It is, thus, the Absolute itself who appears in his own mirror as the diverse universe.

27

Diversity an Apparent Appearance

विज्ञानान्तर्यामिप्राणविराड्देहजातिपिण्डान्ताः।
व्यवहारमात्रमेतत्परमार्थेन तु न सन्त्येव।। २७।।

27. Vijñāna-antaryāmi-prāṇa-virāḍ-
deha-jāti-piṇḍāntaḥ
Vyavahāra-mātrametat
paramārthena tu na santyeva.

Trs.—The flow of fluxional consciousness, the functioning of a single self in all the minds, the (operations) of the (principle) of animation, the appearance of the universal self in all that is (constitutive) of phenomena, the (existence) of forms are either subtle or gross, the (general sense) of species, and finally, the individual existents—all of them may be existing conceptually, but in fact do not exist actually.

Comment—It was Buddha who ushered in the debate that all phenomena, including consciousness, are impermanent, and from this concept of imprmanence conclusion was drawn that everything pertaining to phenomena exists momentarily. This momentary doctrine was so interpreted as to negate the existence of a substantial *ātman* or self. Thus for the Yogācāra school of Asaṅga it was this momentary consciousness that was accorded the semblance of some kind of reality, which is to say that it was real momentarily. The Vedic, or what is called the

Brahmaṇic, tradition is totally opposed to this Buddhist view of momentariness of phenomena. It upholds the metaphysical view that all the changing phenomena are upheld by such a principle which is permanent and substantial—and that principle is termed as the Self or *brahman.* The other doctrine that is adumbrated by some of the Upanishads concerns with the principle of animation. These Upanishads maintain that it is the principle of animation which is identical with the ultimate reality. There are, however, other Upanishads who do not agree with this view of animation. These Upanishads uphold the view that it is the Universal Self that shines in all the phenomenal categories. So it is this Universal Self that is considered as being the ultimate reality.

28-31

Two Kinds of Delusion

रज्ज्वां नास्ति भुजङ्गस्त्रासं कुरुते च मृत्युपर्यन्तम्।
भ्रान्तेर्महती शक्तिर्न विवेक्तुं शक्यते नाम।। २८।।

28. Rajjvām nāsti bhujaṅgas-trāsaṃ
kurute ca mṛtyu-paryantam
Bhrānter mahatī śaktirna
vivektuṃ śakyate nāma.

Trs.—Even the serpent may not be existing in a rope, yet (there is the experience) of such fear, which may (become the cause even) of death. The immense power (which is wielded by the experience) of delusion cannot be explained (rationally) and convincingly.

Comment—Whenevr we have an illusory experience, we are so impacted by the experience as if it is real. When we, for example, have the experience of a rope as being a snake, we are as terrified by the illusory snake as we would be by the actual snake. This process of considering the unreal object as being a real object is the work of ignorance, and ignorance is characterised by the mistaken identification of the real with the unreal. Insofar as illusion lasts, it is experienced as being real. Upon its negation, we come to know that it was an illusion. This unspeakable nature of illusion can never be so formulated as would be rational. It is this irrational nature of illusion that led Śaṁkara to speak of it as being *anirvācanīya.*

तद्वद्धर्माधर्मस्वर्निरयोत्पत्तिमरणसुखदुःखम्।
वर्णाश्रमादि चात्मन्यसदपि विभ्रमबलाद्भवति॥ २९॥

29. Tadvad dharmādharma-svar-nirayotpatti-maraṇa-sukha-duḥkham Varṇāśramādi cātmanyasadapi vibhrama-balād bhavati.

Trs.—Likewise (such) matters as righteousness and unrighteousness, heaven and hell, birth and death, pleasure and pain, social stratification and stages of life, and so on, have no (actual) existence, but shine forth in the self as a mere effect of delusion.

Comment—In this explanation two points need consideration, one is epistemological and the other is ontological. It is assumed *a priori* that whatever we perceive or cognise or ideate has to be evaluated against the background of its reality or unreality. The period during which the illusory perception occurs is experienced as being real, and the question of its ontic unreality does not arise. Likewise all these phenomenal happenings, when viewed from a relative point of view, are taken to be real in the manner illusory happenings are considered to be real. Upon the dawning of knowledge, however, we come to know that what we had perceived in illusion is a trail of unreality. In a similar manner we come to know that the ontological status of phenomena as being unreal when the Absolute is experienced as being non-dual, and apart from the non-dual I-consciousness nothing exists. In this manner the doctrine of illusion helps us to unravel the nature of the Absolute as being non-dual.

एतत्तदन्धकारं यद्भावेषु प्रकाशमानतया।
आत्मानतिरिक्तेष्वपि भवत्यनात्माभिमानोऽयम्॥ ३०॥

30. Etat tadandhakāraṃ yad bhāveṣu prakāśamānatayā

**Ātmānatiriktesvapi bhavatya-
nātmābhimāno'yam.**

Trs.—All the phenomenal entities, on account of delusional darkness, are experienced (or perceived) as being different from (the infinite) self, even though being (essentially) non-different from it due to their appearance within the luminosity of the light of consciousness.

Comment—The Trika considers the essential nature of the Absolute consisting of *prakāśa* and *vimarśa*—the former making the phenomenal entities capable of being manifest, whereas the latter aspect engenders the process of manifestation. An object exists precisely because of its appearance as a reflection within the mirror of consciousness. In the absence of consciousness as light no object has the possiblity of existing, which means that the existing of an object as a manifest entity. Further Trika adheres to the doctrinal principle of the Absolute as being non-dual, which means that the entire objectivity, prior to its manifestation, exists potentially within the Absolute. In this manner is established identity between the macrocosm and microcosm. If it is assumed that everything is non-different from the Absolute, then why this experience of differentiation occurs? Differentiation of phenomena is experienced on a account of the drakness of ignorance, which is identical with the impurity of *māyā* or what is called *māyīyamala*.

तिमिरादपि तिमिरमिदं गण्डस्योपरि महानयं स्फोटः।
यदनात्मन्यपि देहप्राणादावात्ममानित्वम्।। ३१।।

**31. Timirādapi timiramidaṃ
gaṇḍasyopari mahānayaṃ sphotaḥ
yadanātmanyapi deha-prāṇādā-
vātma-mānitvam.**

Trs.—The identification of the self with the not-self (entities) like the ego, the body and the operations of animation is (similar) to the darkness over darkness. It is like a large boil over a tumour.

Comment—The idea that is contained in this verse is as to how ignorance, like darkness, is the main hindrance insofar as self-recognition of one's essential nature is concerned. As we are unable to know who we are on account of ignorance, we thereby identify the self either with the body or *prāṇa* or with ego. Thus ignorance expresses itself in terms of identifying the self with entities that are essentially not-self. It is upon the negation of ignorance that we have the self-recognition in terms of which non-dual identity is established with the Absolute, which means that we are non-different from the Absolute. Thus knowledge consists of in knowing the essential nature of the self, which is to say such knowledge that is opposite to darkness, which is *prākāśa*.

32

The Four Coverings of Ātman

देहप्राणविमर्शनधीज्ञाननभः प्रपञ्चयोगेन।
आत्मानं वेष्टयते चित्रं जालेन जालकार इव।। ३२।।

**32. Deha-prāṇa-vimarśana-dhījñāna-
nabhaḥ-prapañca-yogena
Ātmānaṃ veṣṭayate citraṃ
jālene jāla-kara iva.**

Trs.—What an amazing (experience it is to witness) a silkworm getting restricted inside the self-woven cocoon! (Similar is the case with) a limited being who conceals the nature of the self under the tramendous impact of the feeling (he entertains) with regard to his ego, body, *prāṇa* and conceptual (constructs).

Comment—This verse is the continuation of the preceding one insofar as the concealment of the essential nature of the self is concerned. It is due to the gross covering of the self that leads to the erroneous identification of the self with ego, body and *prāṇa.* The subtle coverings, on the other hand, consist of the manifold cognitions that are given rise to by one's understanding. Insofar as the finer coverings are concerned, they give rise to such feelings of I-ness which are related to the pure but finite consciousness, totally free from subjectivity as well as objectivity. This experience of destitution of thought-constructs may be compared to the void of deep sleep. It is Śiva himself who conceals his essential nature in the process of manifestation. This divine drama of concealment is characterized by the sense wonder.

33

The Removal of Coverings

स्वज्ञानविभवभासनयोगेनोद्वेष्टयेन्निजात्मानम्।
इति बन्धमोक्षचित्रां क्रीडां प्रतनोति परमशिवः।। ३३।।

33. Sva-jñāna-vibhava-bhāsana-
Yogenodveṣṭayennijātmānam
Iti bandha-mokṣacitrām
krīḍām pratanoti Paramaśiva.

Trs.—At times the Lord so releases himself from (the fetters of bondage) as would (facilitate the passage) for the disclosure of his (divine) nature through (the practice of such contemplative) yoga that results in the illumination of the divinity of the nature of self-knowldge. In this manner Paramaśiva enacts the wonderful play of bondage and liberation.

Comment—In contrast to the Advaita Vedānta, Trika is of the view that bondage is not caused by some external agent like *avidyā* or *māyā,* but owes its existence to the divine play of the Lord, which is to say that it is Paramaśiva himself who causes self-bondage. Bondage comes into being when the Absolute so immanantises itself as would be reduced to the status of a finite being (*aṇu*). Were the Absolute not to engage in such an activity, he would be as tranquil or lifeless as is the *brahman* of Śaṁkara. The Absolute is in no way a lifeless entity; rather he is endowed with awareness (*vimarśa*), which means that the

Absolute consists of both *prakāśa* and *vimarśa*. Thus the Godhead of the Absolute expresses itself in such a playful activity as, for example, the enactment of the drama called bondage and release. It is the innate nature of the Absolute to be brimming over with activity, and *kriyā* is one of its powers.

34

The Revelatory Nature of Consciousness

सृष्टिस्थितिसंहारा जाग्रत्स्वप्नौ सुषुप्तमिति तस्मिन्।
भान्ति तुरीये धामनि तथापि तैर्नावृतं भाति।। ३४।।

34. Sṛṣṭi-sthiti-saṁhārā jāgrat-
svapnau suṣuptamiti tasmin
Bhānti turīye dhāmani tathāpi
tair nāvṛtaṃ bhāti.

Trs.—It is within the illuminating (transcendent) Fourth State that (the processes) of emanation, preservation and dissolution are seen to be shining in corresponding states of waking, dreaming and sleeping. These phenomenal states do not remain concealed (in the process) of their appearing.

Comment—The Fourth divine state of consciousness transcends all the temporal structures in such a manner as would not be impacted by the limitations of space and the finitude of time. It is in such a transcendent state of consciousness in which intuitive gnosis is realised with regard to the essential nature of the self. It is as pure as would be possible for it to shine in all the empirical states of consciouness. Free from temporal taints and defilements, it accordingly has the power to witness reality as it is in-itself. No phenomenal entity can obstruct its shining nature precisely because very manifest category is dependent on it. It is, thus, the luminous light of consciousness that illumins everything subjectively as well as objectively. Apart from consciousness, nothing has the possibility of existing.

35

The States of Animation

जाग्रद्विश्वं भेदात्स्वप्नस्तेजः प्रकाशमाहात्म्यात्।
प्राज्ञः सुप्तावस्था ज्ञानघनत्वात्ततः परं तुर्यम्।। ३५।।

35. Jāgrad viśvaṃ bhedāt svapnas tejaḥ prakāśa-māhātmyāt Prājñaḥ suptāvasthā jñāna-ghanatvāt tataḥ paraṃ turyam.

Trs.—(The three empirical states of consciousness are analysed in such a manner as would establish their correlation with the external happenings). Thus the waking state is characterised by diversity, and (accordingly is termed) as being *viśva,* which denotes its universality. (Insofar as) the dreaming state is concerned, it is termed as light (*tejas*) on account of it having the power of manifestation. (Similarly) the sleeping state is (termed as being) *prajñā* (on account its awareness restricted to the self alone). The state of *turya* or the Fourth transcends the three empirical states, and accordingly (it is said to be) a compact mass of knowledge (pertaining to the self). It is such a (divine state) which transcends all (the three) states.

Comment—The manifold perceptions as well as experineces that we have of the world occur in the state of waking. It is for this reason that the waking state is equated to the diversity of diffrrence. In the dreaming state we experience things and objects the way we usually experience in the waking state. This difference between the two states is this, in the waking state experiences occur in a logical sequence, whereas in the dreaming state it is not the case. It is equated to light on account of it having the power to manifest things and experiences. The sleeping state, however, is not totally a state of absence. In this state awareness is at least restricted to the self. Finally, the divine state of the Fourth or *turya* is such a state which transcends all the three empirical states of consciousness. It is a state of divine revelation.

36

The Everlasting Purity of the Absolute

जलधरधूमरजोभिर्मलिनीक्रियते यथा न गगनतलम्।
तद्वन्मायाविकृतिभिरपरामृष्टः परः पुरुषः।। ३६।।

36. Jaladhara-dhūma-rajobhir malinī-
kriyate yathā na gagana-talam
Tadvan-māyā-vikṛtibhiraprā-
mṛṣṭaḥ paraḥ puruṣaḥ.

Trs.—As the surface of the sky is (not touched by such defiling factors as) clouds, smoke and dust, likewise the transcendental self remains untouched by the *māyaic* categories.

Comment—The categories that are caused by *māyā* are the five limiting factors called *kañcukas* or the covering sheaths. These *māyā*-driven factors are responsible in limiting the mental and physical operations of the individual being. However, these five factors, including *māyā* itself, cannot alter the essential nature of the self, because of their shining as reflections within the luminosity of the mirror of consciosness. Whatever operations these limiting factors may be enacting, they do so due to the divine playfulness of the Godhead. What it amounts to saying is that the divinity of Godhead does not undergo any kind of change with regard to its essential nature, even as a limited being. Thus the Godhead of the Absolute continues to be devoid of defilments while manifesting itself in the form of impure categories or phenomena. Thus this theistic absolutism is wonderful and amazing precisely because it does not deprive the Absolute of its divine power.

37

The Psychic Difference among the Contingent Beings

एकस्मिन्घटगगने रजसा व्याप्ते भवन्ति नान्यानि।
मलिनानि तद्वदेते जीवाः सुखदुःखभेदजुषः।। ३७।।

37. Ekasmin ghaṭa-gagane rajasā
vyāpte bhavanti nānyāni
Malināni tadvadete jīvāḥ
sukha-duḥkha-beda-juṣaḥ.

Trs.—The space within a pitcher, upon being (tarnished) by the dust, does not (mean) that the space within other pitchers, too, gets (affected by the taint of the dust). In like manner all the finite beings mutually differ insofar as (the experience) of pain and pleasure is concerned.

Comment—This analogy of space attempts to explain as to why the individual beings differ in the intensity of their empirical experience. The Trika non-dualistic *a priori* assumption maintains that all the finite beings are essentially identical, which is to say that the seeming mutual differences are not grounded in reality. If it is so, then why we see people having variety of experiences, which are redically different from each other? There should not have been eventuating a plethora of experiences. The variety of experiences are occasioned by our past *karman*. However, these mutually differing experiences have no capacity of defiling the purity of the self. As the impurity of a particular space does not defile space in general, so the variety of experiences of the multitude of beings does not affect the purity of the self in any manner.

38

The Appearance of God as Diverse

शान्ते शान्त इवायं हृष्टे हृष्टो विमोहवति मूढः।
तत्त्वगणे सति भगवान्न पुनः परमार्थतः स तथा।। ३८।।

38. Śānte Śānta ivāyam hṛṣte
hṛṣto vimoha-vati mūḍhaḥ
Tattva-gaṇe sati bhagavān na punaḥ
paramārthataḥ sa tathā.

Trs.—The pervasion of the Lord over (various) psychic states (such as) tranquil, happy and deluded manifest (themselves in a such a manner) as if the Divinity were (always) like that, which, in reality, is not the case.

Comment—The esssential nature is changeless. Even when the Lord emanates from itself the pure and impure categories, there occurs no change in his Being. He remains as he is in himself. Insofar as the occurrance of such states as, for exmple, tranquil, happy or delusional are concerned, they entail change, and change denotes the emergence of a new state while causing the destruction of the existing one. The change that we see occurring in things is caused due to the disturbance in the constituents of Nature. The Absolute as transcendent is devoid of constitutents, and so is free from change. However, it appears as if the Absolute is undergoing change when inserting itself in Matter as a finite being.

39-40

Dissolution of Delusion

यदनात्मन्यपि तद्रूपावभासनं तत्पुरा निराकृत्य।
आत्मन्यनात्मरूपां भ्रान्तिं विदलयति परमात्मा।। ३९।।

39. Yadanātmanyapi tadrūpāvabhāsanaṃ
tat purā nirākṛtya
Ātmanyanātma-rūpāṃ bhrāntiṃ
vidalayati paramātmā

Trs.—The Absolute Godhead, while initially shatterring (such ignorance-driven) delusory conceptions as (for example) the identification of the self with the not-self (or with similar) inert substances, afterwards also eradicates (similar) conceptions that (attempt at reducing) the Universal Self to the status of not-self.

Comment—The finite being, though essentially pure and divine, reduces the universality of the Self, due to ignorance, to a state that is characterised by the finitude of limitations. The Divine Self, which essentially is all-time pervasive, omniscient and omnipotent, becomes as finite as to have lost the trajectory of divinity. This finitude expresses itself when a person identifies the essentially divine self with such mental and physical factors as ego, body or *prāṇa.* It is a kind of superimposition of the unreal upon the real. In the case of rope-snake, it is the non-existent snake that is superimposed upon the real rope. Such a misidentification leads to erroneous conclusions. Similarly the not-self entities as, for example, the body or ego are imposed upon the real self, thereby leading to wrong epistemic conclusion in terms of which there occurs misindentification of the self. All this happens because of ignorance. The entire cosmic manifestation is nothing but the self-extension or self-expression of the Absolute, which means that every phenomenal category is permeated by the divine presence. But due to *māyā/avidyā* we consider phenomenality as non-divine, which it is not. However, the Absolute Godhead reveals himself in such a manner as would enable the individual being to realise his essential divinity. The self-revelation of the Lord is called grace. When grace descends upon the aspirant, he thereby is able unshackle himself from the fetters of bondage, and thereby shatter the *māyāic* structures of ignorance. Accordingly does the adept realise the infinite, pure and eternal nature of I-consciousness in terms of which the entire cosmos is appropriated as the self. In this manner is estblished identity between the macrocosm and the microcosm.

इत्थं विभ्रमयुगलकसमूलविच्छेदने कृतार्थस्य।
कर्तव्यान्तरकलना न जातु परयोगिनो भवति।। ४०।।

40. Itthaṃ vibhrama-yugalaka-samūla-
vicchedane kṛtārthasya
Kartavyāntara-kalanā na jātu
parayogino bhavati.

Trs.—A yogi of highest (spiritual state), while having depleted both types of delusion, remains inwardly so content as to have nothing (further) to accomplish.

Comment—The two types of delusion from which a finite individual suffers, according to the Trika, is, firstly, of identifying the self with ego, body and *prāṇa* and secondly, from the error of taking the not-self as the self. These two types of delusion are, as it were, the *sine qua non* of phenomenal existence. As a consequence of this, the finite being always experiences life in terms of unfulifilled aspirations. Thus he is caught up in the wheel of becoming. A yogi, on the other, having crossed the ocean of delusion in the boat of knowledge, realises everything that he has to realise. There remains nothing further for him to accomplish.

41-42

Dissolution of Diversity

पृथिवी प्रकृतिर्माया त्रितयमिदं वेद्यरूपतापतितम्।
अद्वैतभावनबलाद्भवति हि सन्मात्रपरिशेषम्।। ४१।।

41. Pṛthvī prakṛtir māyā tritayamidam vedya-rūpatā-patitam Advaita-bhāvana-balād bhavati hi sanmātra-pariśeṣam.

Trs.—On account of the power of non-dual contemplation there (eventuates) the reduction of the triad of objectivity, (embodied) by Earth, Nature and Māyā, to the basic form of existence, consisting of purity and simplicity.

Comment—On account of ignorance we consider our cognitions and perceptions to be embodying the truthful picture of the seen. Whetever we perceive, we perceive it the way it appears to us. It is the way a thing or event appears that is considered to be the actual picture of the appearing object. Our knowledge, thus, is restricted to the surface of the object, which means that we have no notion or idea as to what an object is in-itself. It is for this reason that the *Śivasūtra* spoke of such empirical forms of knowledge as being the source of bondage. Instead of releasing one from the fetters of bondage, empirical knowledge, on the contrary, binds one to the bondage of limitations. When this principle of analysis is applied to the triad of Earth, Nature and

Māyā, we comprehend them in terms of their effect, which means that we do not know them as they are in themselves. It is the data that our senses produce that becomes the basis of our knowledge. Sense-driven knowledge has no possibility of providing such knowledge which represents things as they are in themselves. The only way of arriving at knowledge that is truly truthful is by following the contemplative path of non-dualism.

रशनाकुण्डलकटकं भेदत्यागेन दृश्यते यथा हेम।
तद्वद्भेदत्यागे सन्मात्रं सर्वमाभाति।। ४२।।

42. raśanā-kuṇḍala-kaṭakam bheda-
tyāgena dṛśyate yathā hema
Tadvad bheda-tyāge sanmātraṃ
sarvamābhāti.

Trs.—(The different transformations) of gold (in the form) of ornaments like girdle, earring, bangle, etc. will appear as simple gold (only when their) differentiating (nomenclature) is eliminated. Likewise will phenomena shine in a simple and pure form of existence upon the removal of differentiating factors.

Comment—Prior to the transformation of gold into different forms and shapes, the slab of gold exists in such a state that actually pertains to the whole. This state of its purity, however, is disturbed once the process of transformation is intiated, which means that gold accordingly changes its character and thereby loses its purity and simplicity. The original state of purity of gold can be restored when different ornaments are reduced to the simple state of unity in terms of which differentiating factors are eliminated. It is by melting the ornaments in the burining fire that the state of unity is realised. Likewise is the case with phenomena. The phenomenal diversity can be reduced to simple unity of oneness with Paramaśiva if the prescribed contemplative path of Trika yoga is cultivated.

43

The Nature Brahman

तद्ब्रह्म परं शुद्धं शान्तमभेदात्मकं समं सकलम्।
अमृतं सत्यं शक्तौ विश्राम्यति भास्वरूपायाम्।। ४३।।

43. tad brahma paraṃ śuddhaṃ
śāntamabhedātmakaṃ samaṃ sakalaṃ
Amṛtaṃ satyaṃ śaktau
viśrāmayati bhāsvarūpāyām.

Trs.—That *brahman,* (who is Absolute), is transcendent, and (accordingly is the embodiment) of purity and tranquility, and (as a) non-dual reality (expresses itself) evenly as everything. (This Absolute) is both real and immortal, and (as such) reposes on its own Śakti which is of the nature of consciousness.

Comment—The Absolute is termed as being transcendent precisely because it is beyond the debilitating effects of *māyā*, which is to say that temporality cannot touch it. It is pure because it is not tainted by imuprities, and so is devoid of defilements. It is tranquil in its *prakāśa* aspect, and so is free from fractious causing-disturbances. The Absolute of the Trika is non-dual, as nothing exists apart from it. As nondual Reality, everything exists within it in the same manner as does the colourful plummage exist in the juice of the peacock's egg, which means that it is the Absolute itself who is homogenously everything. The Absolute is immortal because it is eternal, which is to say that there occurs no depletion in its nature. Since it is unborn, it is not subject to birth, old age and death. Accordingly the Absolute is changeless. It is true because it alone truly exists freely. It reposes on its Śakti because it is not only *prakāśa,* but is also *vimarśa.* It is at this point that the Absolute of Trika differs from that of Advaita Vedānta, in that it is endowed with such power as Free Will, which theologically is denoted by the term Śakti.

44

Brahman as the Source of Phenomena

इष्यत इति वेद्यत इति सम्पाद्यत इति च भास्वरूपेण।
अपरामृष्टं यदपि तु नभः प्रसूनत्वमभ्येति।। ४४।।

44. Īṣyata iti vedyata iti sampādyata
iti ca bhāsvarūpeṇa
Aparāmrṣṭam yadapi tu
nabhaḥ-prasūnatvamabhyeti.

Trs.—Whatever is willed or perceived or constructed will be like a sky flower if not illuminated by consciousness.

Comment—Trika views the Absolute as being of the nature of consciousness, and consciousness is said to consist of the illuminative light and awareness. Were consciousness to be devoid of *prakāśa,* there would be no knowable, which, in other words, means that everything in the universe, including the universe, have the characteristics of being known on account of *prakāśa.* Thus a thing has the capacity to manifest itself because of it being the congealed form of consciousness. There is nothing in the universe that can be said to be existing apart from consciousness. Were that be the case, then the existence of things would be same as is of the sky flower, which is to say that they would be non-existent. It is, thus, the light of consciousness which makes a thing to exist. Absence of the light of consciousness would entail the non-existence of a thing. Things exist because they shine in the illuminative consciousness as objects. It all amounts to saying that whatever is willed or perceived or constructed becomes manifest on account of consciousness.

45

Interior Emanation

शक्तित्रिशूलपरिगमयोगेन समस्तमपि परमेशो।
शिवनामनि परमार्थे विसृज्यते देवदेवेन।। ४५।।

45. Śakti-triśūla-parigama-yogena
samastamapi parameśe
Śivanāmani paramārthe
visṛjyate devadevena.

Trs.—The Supreme Lord, while making the use of the triad of powers, initially gives rise to the entire phenomena through (such) divine and eternally existing aspect which is known as Śiva.

Comment—The Godhead of the Absloute is said to be endowed with such innate powers as *ichhā-śakti, jñāna-śakti* and *kriyā-śakti* corresponding to the conative, cognitive and creative powers. The trident as a symbol is so made use of as to represent these three powers of will, knowledge and action, which, according to the Trika thought, constitute the essential nature of Śiva. As and when Śiva becomes aware of his divine powers, he accordingly is so inclined as to give rise to the manifest categories that are constitutive of phenomena. This creative urgency towards manifestation of categories of the Lord is described in terms of the visibility of handling the triad of powers through the symbol of trident. It is the *icchā-śakti* or the conative power of the Lord which initially initiates the process of emanation of the phenomena. Prior to the externalisation of manifestation, Śiva initially accomplishes this creative task within his own interior Being. The emanation of a particular phenomenon denotes the awareness of the object that is to be emanated. It means that emanation of the object cannot occur apart from awareness. The initial appearance of the object occurring within Śiva is on account of his cognitive power. Upon the appearance of the object within Śiva, there then occurs the actual externalisation of the object, which is accomplished by the creative power of *kriyā-śakti*. Similar process of making objects is even followed by human beings prior to the actual making of the object. The architect, for example, initially wills that the object has to be made, and then conceives its format, and finally, makes the object. Thus the making of the object ivolves the process in terms of which subjectively willed, conceived and constructed object is so externalised as would facilitate its actual making.

46

External Manifestation

पुनरपि च पञ्चशक्तिप्रसरणक्रमेण बहिरपि तत्।
अण्डत्रयं विचित्रं सृष्टं बहिरात्मलाभेन।। ४६।।

46. Punarapi ca pañca-śakti-prasaraṇa-kramena bahirapi tat
Aṇḍa-trayaṃ vicitraṃ sṛṣṭam bahirātma-lābhena.

Trs.—The next step that the Lord took in emanating externally (the amazingly) wonderful three spheres (of Māyā, Prakṛti and Earth) (and in terms of which) he (the Lord) also manifested himself outwardly along with five divine powers.

Comment—The five innate divine powers of the Absolute Godhead are the uncontaminated consciousness (*cit*), blissfulness (*ānanda*), free will (*icchā*), power of cognition or knowledge (*jñāna*) and, finally, creative power (*kriyā*). All these five powers constitute the essential nature of the Absolute Godhead. They operate in such a manner as to be identical with him. The external manifestation of these powers occur in terms of them being reflected in the form of three spheres of Māyā, Prakṛti and Earth representing the causal, subtle and gross aspects of the emanated objectivity. This entire process of emanation of manifestation demonstrates the wonderful dexterity of the Lord. Thus whatever is manifested externally expresses as well as embodies the essential nature of the Lord. While giving rise to the external manifestation, the Lord thereby discovers himself in this projected emanation, and that constitutes his external self or, should we say, *bahirātma-lābha.*

47-50

The Process of Self-realisation

इति शक्तिचक्रयन्त्रं क्रीडायोगेन वाहयन्देवः।
अहमेव शुद्धरूपः शक्तिमहाचक्रनायकपदस्थः।। ४७।।

47. Iti śakti-cakra-yantraṃ kriḍā-
yogena vāhayan devaḥ
Ahameva śuddha-rūpaḥ śakti-mahā-
cakra-nāyaka-padasthaḥ

Trs.—It is I myself, the Lord, while putting into motion the machine of the wheel of divine powers, is characterised by (such nature) as is pure, is situated at the highest level, functions as a master hero of the infinite circle of energies of divine powers.

Comment—The practitioner of the path of Trika yoga, through the process of deepening off absorption (*samāveśa*), has the realisation that he is no more a limited being, but basically is divine in nature, possessing infinite divine powers. Realising his identity with the Absolute, the *sādhaka* has the knowledge of himself as being the sole master hero of numerous powers, and these divine powers represent what may be called the herions to the hero. Within himself, the yogi experiences that it is he who is activating these powers playfully, and the primary powers being *cit, ānanda, icchā, jñāna* and *kriyā*. These powers through the process of unification appear in every individual in the form of twelve "energies," known as the *śakticakra*. This circle of powers is represented by the twelve Kālīs. As energies, the Kālīs absorb the mental activities or processes of all the subjects.

मय्येव भाति विश्वं दर्पण इव निर्मले घटादीनि।
मत्तः प्रसरति सर्वं स्वप्नविचित्रत्वमिव सुप्तात्।। ४८।।

48. Mayyeva bhāti viśvaṃ darpaṇa iva nirmale ghaṭādini
Mattaḥ prasarati sarvaṃ svapna-vicitratvamiva suptāt.

Trs.—An adept of the Trika path has this experience which explains the depth of non-duality. The adept says: "The entire universe appears or shines within (the luminosity of my consciousness) in the same manner as do objects like a pitcher, etc., appear in a clean mirro. (Likewise) everything proceeds from me like the flux of manifold dreams that flow out from a dreaming person."

Comment—A true and athentic Trika yogin experiences his non--dual divinity in such a manner as if the entirety of phenomenon is the reflection of his own divine powers. He experiences the categories of existence emanating from his own divine self. This flowing out of the categories is, analogously speaking, analysed in terms of the emanation of dreams from a dreaming person or in terms of reflection occurring in a mirror that is free from such contamination as impurity inflicts upon the finite being.

अहमेव विश्वरूपः करचरणादिस्वभाव इव देहः।
सर्वस्मिन्नहमेव स्फुरामि भावेषु भास्वरूपमिव।। ४९।।

49. Ahameva viśva-rūpaḥ kara-caraṇādi-svabhāva iva dehaḥ
Sarvasminnahameva sphurāmi bhāveṣu bhāsvarūpamiva.

Trs.—Further says the yogi of the highest realisation: "As it is the (basic) innate nature of the body (to be so constructed) as to have limbs like hands, feet, etc., so (likewise) the entire phenomena (should be seen) as my own form (in the same manner) as the shimmering of light occurs in all the existing entities, (which is to say) that I shine as light in all (the forms) of existence."

Comment—The use of the image of the body and its limbs demonstrates the unity of the whole in the midst of diversity represented by the bodily limbs. The body is one and whole, yet it consists of limbs, which embody duality. The phenomenal entities cannot become manifest unless they shine within the light of I-consciousness, which is to say that it is the light of *ātman* which endows existence to such existents that appear or manifest themselves. The Trika system of thought maintains that all objectivity is nothing but the congealment of the light of consciousness in the manner of reflection. In other words, it means that the objective existents are the form of consciousness. The purpose of such argument is to demonstrate the truth of the metaphysical *a priori* assertions of the Trika thought.

द्रष्टा श्रोता घ्राता देहेन्द्रियवर्जितोऽप्यकर्तापि।
सिद्धान्तागमतर्कांश्चित्रानहमेव रचयामि।। ५०।।

50. Draṣṭā śrotā ghrātā dehendriya-varjito'pyakartāpi
Siddhāntāgama-tarkāṃścitrān-ahameva racayāmi.

Trs.—Even though I may be devoid of (physical) body, senses, and may not (accordingly) be performing (mental or physical) deeds, yet it is I alone who sees, hears, smells as well as composes (exceedingly) wonderful (texts) on Śāstras like Siddhāntas, Āgamas and treatises on Logic.

Comment—The *ātman* or the Self, according to the Trika, is of the nature of pure consciousness, which means that nothing has the power to taint or defile it. The very first *sūtra* of the *Śivasūtra* speaks of consciousness to be the Self (*caitanyaṃ ātmā*).

The Self as pure consciousness is such a viewpoint which adumbrates an idea that nothing can restrict the inclusivity of consciousness. Consciousness per say, therefore, transcends such structures that are inert like the body and the senses. These material entities receive the power of performing their respective functions from consciousness. It amounts to saying that consciousness, which is the Self, may be destitute of such material aspects as body and senses, yet it is consciousness as I that is the real seer who sees, is the real hearer who hears, is the real composer who composes texts and treatises of various kinds. Thus the Trika thinkers coined such a term as I-consciousness that would express the real meaning of the Self as consciousness.

51-52

The Dissolution of Desultory Misery

इत्थं द्वैतविकल्पे गलिते प्रविलङ्घ्य मोहनीं मायाम्।
सलिले सलिलं क्षीरं क्षीरमिव ब्रह्मणि लयी स्यात्॥ ५१॥

51. Itthaṃ dvaita-vikalpe galite
pravilaṅghya mohanīṃ māyām
Salile salilam kṣīre kṣīramiva
brahmaṇi layīsyāt.

Trs.—Upon the dissolution of dualistic conceptual (framework), (and when) an individual being, while crossing over the (barriers) of Māyā, immerses in *brahman* in the manner of water becoming one with water and milk with milk.

Comment—Insofar as an individual being is held hostage by three impurities of *āṇava, māyīya* and *kārma,* there exists no possibility for him to be free from such cognitions and experiences that are characterised by difference. It is *māyīya* impurity that is responsible in generating a conceptual framework that is deeply rooted in the soil of difference. It is the mind that, as it were, authenticates dualism through the medium of ideas. However, the dualistic barriers can be overcome provided we cultivate the path of Trika yoga and philosophy. By cultivating such a visionary path an individual has the possibility of actualising the non-dualistic experience in terms of which the framework of difference is dissolved in the same manner as is complete unity affected when water dissolves itself into water or milk into milk. This analogy is used to show as to how the process of unity with *brahman* is realised.

इत्थं तत्त्वसमूहे भावनया शिवमयत्वमभियाते।
कः शोकः को मोहः सर्वं ब्रह्मावलोकयतः।। ५२।।

52. Ittham tattva-samūhe bhāvanayā
Śiva-mayatvamabhiyāte
Kaḥ śokaḥ ko mohaḥ sarvaṃ
brahmāvalokayataḥ.

Trs.—For a yogin what can exist (in the form) of sorrow or delusion (when) h sees everything as being (the form) of *brahman* (and in terms of which) the entirety of multitude of categories have been (experienced) as having attained (perfect) unity of oneness with Śiva through the process of absorptive contemplation.

Comment—Insofar as an individual being remains under the impact of differentiating conceptual framework, there is bound to occur the emergence of such an experience that will be of the nature of delusion or sorrow. An individual experiences sorrow as a result of delusion, and delusion is characterised in considering the unreal to be the real, as in the case of the illusion of rope being seen as a snake. However, the moment a yogi sees or experiences *brahman* to be the sole reality, there accordingly eventuates the disappearance of all forms of sorrow. It means that the *sādhaka* has such an experience in terms of which the entirety of categories are dissolved into the ultimate source from which they proceed. There are, thus, two movements in Śiva which are known as *unmeṣa* and *nimeṣa*—the former representing manifestation and the latter dissolution. When both these movement are experienced, there dawns such recognitive knowledge in terms of which is restored the repose of unity of Being. This experience of unity with Śiva ensues when the path of *jñānayoga,* known as *bhāvaña*, is followed and practised.

53-54

Karman as the Cause of Rebirth

कर्मफलं शुभमशुभं मिथ्याज्ञानेन संगमादेव।
विषमो हि संगदोषस्तस्करयोगोऽप्यतस्करस्येव॥ ५३॥

53. Karma phalaṃ śubhamaśubhaṃ
mithyā-jñānena saṅgamādeva
Viṣamo hi saṅga-doṣas-taskara-
yogo'pyataskarasyeva.

Trs.—It is due to the association with erroneous knowledge that a person has to reap both good and evil fruits of his deeds. (One should have no doubt) with regard to the dangerous consequences of evil association. (Association with evil may be seen to be of the same nature) as would be the association of an honest person with a thief.

Comment—A deed, whether good or evil, is performed in and through the sense-organs initiated by the mind through the psycho-physical construct called ego. However, it is the divine force that both visibly and invisibly wills the actions that are performed by an individual. It is a doctrine of divine determinate causality that is what is enunciated. Instead of looking at our actions as proceeding from the divine, we as limited individuals, on account of ignorance, view the performance of deeds as having emanated from the ego. Thinking of deeds as being personal, so accordingly we feel responsible for the deeds that we have performed. If, on the contrary, we look at deeds as being divinely determined, we shall thereby avoid the sense of guilt.

लोकव्यवहारकृतां य इहाविद्यामुपासते मूढाः।
ते यान्ति जन्ममृत्यू धर्माधर्मार्गलावद्धाः।। ५४।।

54. Loka-vyavahāra-kṛtām ya ihāvidyām-upāsate muḍhāḥ
Te yānti janma-mṛtyu dharmādharmārgalā-baddhāḥ.

Trs.—Such deluded people (suffer from) the repeated cycle of births and deaths who, (on the one hand), are so attached to erroneous knowledge (as would) determine (the entirety) of their worldly activities and, (on the other hand), are fettered by the chain of deeds that are either good or sinful.

Comment—Most of the worldly activities of a man of ignorance are performed within a cognitive framework that is erroneous. A knowledge that is erroneous does not mean total absence of knowledge; rather it signifies such deficiency of knowledge as would indicate its incompleteness. It means that man is not completely destitute of knowledge. Whatever knowledge he may have, it is so incomplete as to be full of errors, which means that it is non-actionable. Erroneous knowledge is similar to the knowledge that we have under illusory conditions. Thus whatever deeds we do in the state of incomplete knowledge would evidently lead to the performance of such actions whose fruits would be either pleasant or unpleasant. Instead of redeeming man from his conditioned existence, such deeds lead to further conditioning. This conditioning of existence results in what is called the cycle of repeated births and deaths.

55-56

Dysfucntionality of Karman

अज्ञानकालनिचितं धर्माधर्मात्मकं तु कर्मापि।
चिरसंचितमिव तूलं नश्यति विज्ञानदीप्तिवशात्।। ५५।।

55. Ajñāna-kāla-nicitaṃ dharmādharmā-tmakaṃ tu karmāpi
Cira-sañcitamiva tūlaṃ naśyati vijñāna-dīpti vaśāt.

Trs.—The sinful deeds that get accumulated during such period when ignorance persists for long (and equally) gets destroyed like the heaps of cotton when the blazing flame of light (is lit) by wisdom.

Comment—*Jñāna* is such a form of wisdom of reality that is obtained through the study of holy writing, whereas *vijñāna* is knowledge that is dependent upon life-experience. It is possible for a person to be completely convinced intellectually insofar as truthfulness of Trika absolutism is concerned, but at the level-of-life-experience may be experiencing such existential finitude in terms of which the difference between God and man becomes unbridgeable. What we learn intellectually has to be so inserted into our life-experiences as would become natural part of it. Such a situation of natural experience of non-difference is realised when perfect *samāveśa* with the Divine is realised.

ज्ञानप्राप्तौ कृतमपि न फलाय ततोऽस्य जन्म कथम्।
गतजन्मबन्धयोगो भाति शिवार्कः स्वदीधितिभिः।। ५६।।

56. Jñāna-prāptau kṛtamapi na phalāya tato'sya janma katham Gata-janma-bandha-yogo bhāti Śivārkaḥ sva-dīdhitibhiḥ.

Trs.—Deeds do not fructify for a person who performs them after having attained (the perfect state) of error free knowledge. How, therfore, can there be rebirth for him? (Such a person is) sun-like Śiva who, while shining eternally (in the form) of divine rays, has completely destroyed fetters of bondage.

Comment—The theory of *karman* is so used causally as to explain rationally the rebirth of a dead person, which means that life does not come to an end at the time of death. The causal aspect of the theory consists of in the assertion that each deed of a person bears a corresponding fruit. From a large perspective it would mean that our form of existence is determined by the kind of actions we have done in previous lives. All our experiences, therefore, are the result of deeds done in our previous lives. It is this causal chain that is broken by a Shaiva yogin, which means that the yogin has so freed himself from the *karman*-causality as to be no more subject to the cyclic chain of becoming in terms of births and deaths. It also means that the deeds that a yogin presently performs have no power or capacity to bear the required fruit. A yogi either realises complete freedom while alive or after death: the former kind of liberation is known as *jīvan-mukti* and the latter type as *videhi-mukti*. Such a yogin is truly Śiva in the sense of having realised complete immersion in the essential being of the Absolute. Such a yogin is no less than the sun. As the rays of the sun destroy darkness everywhere, likewise a Shaiva yogin, through the spritual rays of enlightenment, obliterates every form of darkness of ignorance.

57-59

Freedom from the Pain of Rebirth

तुषकम्बुककिंशारुकमुक्तं बीजं यथाङ्कुरं कुरुते।
नैव तथाणवमायाकर्मविमुक्तो भवाङ्कुरं ह्यात्मा।। ५७।।

57. Tuṣa-kumbuka-kiṃśāruka-muktaṃ
bījam yathāṅkuraṃ kurute
Naiva tathāṇava-māyā-karma-
vimukto bhavāṅkuraṃ hyātmā.

Trs.—When the husk and the inner yellowish covering as well as the germ of the paddy seed are removed, it no more (has the capacity) to sprout into a seedling. Likewise when (the coverings) of (three) impurities of contraction (*āṇava-mala*), of difference (*māyīya-mala*) and of the past deeds (*kārma-mala*) are removed from an individual being, (there)does not eventuate (furthr births) for the *ātman*.

Comment—The analogy of paddy grain is used to explain as to how the *karman*-generated causality in relation to the becoming process of an individual being can be made dysfunctional. Insofar as the paddy grain has the protection of the coverings, it accordingly possesses the power of giving birth to a new seedling, which means that causality is fully operational. Once these covering are removed, the paddy grain loses its capacity to give birth to a new seedling, or should we say that the paddy obtains freedom from the becoming process. While applying this rule to a finite being, it means that insofar as the coverings in the form of impurities exist, there will be no end to the process of endlss becoming of births and deaths. It is upon realising the absolute identity with the Absolute that the yogi is able to destroy completely the coverings of impurities, which result in the immediate fredom from the bondage of rebirth. It is the aim of a Shaiva yogi to attain this ultimate liberative state of unity through the destruction impurities—and in this attainment is realised the ultimate soteriological goal, which is liberation from bondage.

आत्मज्ञो न कुतश्चन बिभेति सर्वं हि तस्य निजरूपम्।
नैव च शोचति यस्मात्परमार्थे नाशिता नास्ति।। ५८।।

58. Ātmajño na kutaścana bibheti
sarvaṃ hi tasya nija-rūpaṃ
Naiva ca śocati yasmāt
paramārthe nāśitā nāsti.

Trs.—A self-realised person does not experience fear of any kind whatsoever (on account of him having recognised) everything as being his own essential form. He also does not experience grief due to the fact (of him having known) that neither death nor destruction exist (in reality)

Comment—Insofar as an individual being considers itself as being limited as well as different from everything, he is bound to experience both mental and physical fear. The emergence of fear is a prelude to what may be called existential desertion. It is the other, whether in physical or mental realm, that is seen as a threat to one's wellbeing. On account of constant threat from the other, there emerges anxiety that drives out every bit of energy, which results in the experience of despair. In the case of the realised person, there does not hang any dagger of threat. It is so because he sees, in the words of the *Gītā*, everything in himself and himself in everything. Further, a realised person does not experience grief on account of him having known that neither death nor destruction exist, and this doctrine of non-dual non-death has been beautifully explained in the second chapter of the *Bhagavadgītā*.

अतिगूढहृदयगञ्जप्ररूढपरमार्थरत्नसंचयतः ।
अहमेवेति महेश्वरभावे का दुर्गतिः कस्य।। ५९।।

59. Ati-gūḍha-hṛdaya-gañja-prarūḍha-paramārtha-ratna-sāñcayataḥ
Ahameveti maheśvara-bhāve kā durgatiḥ kasya.

Trs.—What can be viewed as a kind of misfortune and for whom when, in fact, heaps of (valuable) jewels of the Absolute are so accumulated as to lie hidden within the interior treasures-house of the self and in terms of which is realised Godhead as being one's own essential nature.

Comment—Despair, fear and dread seem to be natural allies of an individual being. Insofar as the individualised consciousness considers itself as being contracted and different from every entity, there is bound to occur the sense of fear and in terms of which everything other than oneself becomes the source of existential anxiety. This anxiety terminates in the rise of nihilistic values, and accordinagly life is seen either absurd or meaningless. Contrary to this negative view, the Trika, while affirming life, uses hope as certainty. It affirms life as a meaningful project when it doctrinally asserts that nothing exists apart from the Divine, which is to say that we as embodied beings are non-different from the Absolute, and accordingly neither die nor are we subject to destruction. We exist as divine waves in the ocean of Divinity. This aspect of self is beautifully explained in the second chapter of the *Bhagavadgītā*.

60

Nature of Liberation

मोक्षस्य नैव किंचिद्धामास्ति न चापि गमनमन्यत्र।
अज्ञानग्रन्थिभिदा स्वशक्त्यभिव्यक्तता मोक्षः।। ६०।।

60. mokṣasya naiva kiñcid dhāmāsti
na cāpi gamanamanyatra
ajñāna-granthi-bhidā sva-śaktya-
bhivyaktatā mokṣaḥ.

Trs.—The state of (soteriological) freedom (from bondage) does not have a specific abode (like the abode of Viṣṇu or Śiva) nor is it characterised by an upward movement towards some (celestial abode). Absolute freedom is of the nature of self-illumination and in terms of which one's divine energy is realised, and (accordingly) the knots of ignorance are removed.

Comment—Usually people think that the state of liberation must necessarily possess a definite location in space. Such thinking with regard to liberation is entertained on account of the fact that nothing exists without a basis or locus. There must be some support or locus for an object to exist. This kind of anthromorophic thinking, however, is inapplicable to the absolute freedom on account of it being transcendent. The transcendent freedom connot be explained simply in such a conceptual framework which is driven by temporality. It is for this reason that the absolute freedom is said to be nothing else than the illumination of one's essential nature, and upon its revelation the knots of ignorance also find their final resolution.

61

Moral Life and Liberation

भिन्नाज्ञानग्रन्थिर्गतसन्देहः पराकृतभ्रान्तिः।
प्रक्षीणपुण्यपापो विग्रहयोगेऽप्यसौ मुक्तः।। ६१।।

61. Bhinnājñāna-granthir gatasandehaḥ parākṛta-bhrāntiḥ
Prakṣīṇa-puṇya-pāpo vigraha-yoge'pyasau muktaḥ.

Trs.—The (state of liberation) is realised by a person upon the removal of the knots of ignorance, which (is characterised) by the sense of difference, (as well as) upon the removal of doubts and delusion which (at the same time) result in the complete dissolution both of righteousness and unrighteousness.

Comment—A person will remain in the state of bondage to the extent the emergence of freedom-giving knowledge is prevented by the goiter-like knots of three impurities and the Māyā-generated sheaths. On account of ignorance, an individual being identifies his self either with the body or with the constructed ego. The other tendency of ignorance is to identify his body or ego with the self. It is this erroneous identification of the self that results in bondage, and bondage is characterised by the endless cycle of rebirths. This entire gamut of rebirths, and thereby of ignorance-generated knots, become dysfunctional the moment the soteric knowledge of non-duality emrges, which means the complete devouring of polar or dialectical conceptual framework. It is what constitutes such knowledge as would transcend the three empirical states of consiousness by ushering in the Fourth, which is identical with liberation.

62

Non-Functionality of Karman

अग्न्यभिदग्धं बीजं यथा प्ररोहासमर्थतामेति।
ज्ञानाग्निदग्धमेवं कर्म न जन्मप्रदं भवति।। ६२।।

62. Agnyabhidagdham bījaṃ yathā
prarohāsamarthatāmeti
jñānāgni-dagdhamevaṃ
karma na janma-pradam bhavati.

Trs.—As the seed, when parched in fire, losses its capacity (to germinate as well as) to grow, likewise (the present and the past) actions of a person lose the capacity of causing (the future cycle) of rebirths upon being consummed by the fire of (recognitive) knowledge (of the self).

Comment—This verse explains such process as would make the causal aspect of our deeds useless. A *sādhaka* has to so purify itself in the fire of knowledge in such a manner as would be free from the defilements of difference as well as of limitations. It is in the ascetical fire of *sādhanā* that the salvific knowledge is generated, which terminates in making the causal aspect of action inoperational. Thus, liberation from bondage, characterised by self-recognition, is arduous but not impossible. As Lallā would say, in one of her verses, that the gold gains its absolute purity when all impurities are completely burnt in the burning fire. It is this very principle that applies to us. A finite being will abandon the garb of finitude when all the impurities are burnt in the ascetically-generating heat of self-recognition.

63

Impressions as the Cause of Transmigration

परिमितबुद्धित्वेन हि कर्मोचितभाविदेहभावानया।
संकुचिता चितिरेतद्देहध्वंसे तथा भवति।। ६३।।

63. Parimita-buddhitvena hi karmocita-
bhāvi-deha-bhāvanayā
Saṅkucitā-citireted-deha-dhvaṃse
tathā bhavati.

Trs.—The limited individual being, while (firmly) fixed with such a conceptual (framework) that considers the self as being limited, traverses (such path) due to the impressions of the future body, whose formation happens in accordance with the deeds that it has performed, to the resultant situation upon the end of the current form.

Comment—The impression that owe their existence to our deeds and thoughts give imperceptibly rise to such inclinations or attitudes that are responsible, upon the end of the present form of existence, in giving birth to such forms of life that would bear the consequences of deeds previously done. The present state of existence, whether good or bad, owes its existence to the deeds that have been done previously, which means that the present form of existence is the result of the fruit of past deeds. In this manner is established the causal relationship between *karman* and its fruit, which, when analysed, would mean that a deed is the cause and fruit (existence) is the result. Thus the ancient saying: As you sow, so shall you yeap—bears its appropriate fruit within the framework of causality.

64-66

Liberation upon the Dissolution of Impressions

यदि पुनरमलं बोधं सर्वसमुत्तीर्णबोद्धृकर्तृमयम्।
विततमनस्तमितोदितभारूपं सत्यसंकल्पम्।। ६४।।
दिक्कालकलनविकलं ध्रुवमव्ययमीश्वरं सुपरिपूर्णम्।
बहुतरशक्तिव्रातप्रलयोदयविरचनैककर्तारम्।। ६५।।

**64. Yadi punaramalaṃ bodhaṃ sarva-
samuttīrṇa-bodhṛ-kartṛ-mayam
Vitatamanasatamitodita-bhā-
rūpaṃ satya saṅkalpam.**

**65. Dikkāla-kalana-vikalaṃ dhruvama-
vyayamīśvaraṃ suparipūrṇam
Bhautara-śakti-vrāta-pralayodaya-
viracanaika-kartāram.**

Trs.—As to how (its can be maintained) that a person is (engaged) in the movement of rebirths when he firmly is (convinced) of the knowledge and feels perfectly that (he is none other than) the pure consciousness, (and this consciousness is said to be) the "knower" and "doer" (of everything) at such a state where all phenomena are transcended, and (which is also) infinite, and it is (so characterised as to denote) both dissolution and emergence of the light (of I-consciousness), (and whose) will always bears fruit (on account of it being) free from such concepts as space and time, (which means that I-consciousnes) is eternal, free from change, and so (accordingly) is powerful and perfect in every respect. It is this (all-powerful consciousness) which has the power of bringing about the rise and fall of a host of divine powers and which (consciousness is identical) with Śiva, and who is a perfect master of all the divine activities concerning the emanated objectivity. (There is no localised place) from where and towards which it, viz. infinite consciousness, can move.

Comment—The question that is posed in these verses is as to how it is possible for the Absolute, who is philosophically proposed to be transcendent and changeless, to undergo the process of becoming in terms of rebirth? The process of becoming involves change, and if the Absolute undergoes change through transmigration, it would mean that It is not full, whole and without parts, and so would be considered as temporal as any phenomenal object. It is at this point that the Trika finds the solution through its theory of ignorance and reflection. Insofar as an individual is wrapped by the sheaths of impurities and *kāñcukas* of Māyā, there will continue the occurrence of such erroneous knowledge which will result in the mis-identification of the self with the body or with the constructed ego or with entities that are said to be not-self. Such-like questions will disappear the moment the adept transcends the three empirical states of consciousness by ushering in into the Fourth in which occurs the revelation with regard to the divine nature of the self. Thus the adept realises that Paramaśiva in its descent towards self-manifestation as the objective universe eventuates in the manner of a reflection in a mirror, which means that the unity and wholeness of the Absolute in no manner is affected. The experience of identity of the macrocosm and the microcosm eliminates every kind of differentiating misconception and in terms of which accordingly is established as to what constitutes the real nature of the absolute self.

सृष्ट्यादिविधिसुवेधसमात्मानं शिवमयं विबुद्धेत।
कथमिव संसारी स्याद्वितस्य कुतः क्व वा सरणम्।। ६६।।

66. Sṛṣṭyādi-vidhi-suvedhasamātmānaṃ
Śiva-mayaṃ vibhuddhyeta
Kathamiva saṃsārī syād
vitatasya kutaḥ kva vā saraṇam.

Trs.—(Logically how is it possible to say that) such a person (can be subject) to transmigration who knows himself to be pure I-consciousness, which is (at the same time) the absolute knower and doer at the plane of transcendence, and thereby whose will always is so fruitful as to be (totally) free from space-time concepts, which (means that) it is devoid of change, is omniscient and omnipotent, and as such causes the rise and fall of multitude of divine powers and which is Śiva, and accordingly is the master of all such functions that pertain to the emanation of objectivity? From where and to which place can such an infinite power move?

Comment—This verse explains the transcendent aspect of the absolute truth, which is to say that we cannot explain such reality in terms of concepts that owe their existence to the conditioned mode of existence, determined by the determinate causality. A true Shaiva contemplative realises that the Absolute alone is the truth, and I as the *sādhaka* am non-different from that truth. Realising the unfathomable nature of truth, the *sādhaka* does not thereby pigeon-hole conceptually the Absolute as this or that. Freedom from thought-constructs results in the destruction of such dispositions that give rise to the cycle of becoming in the form of a continuous series of rebirths.

67

Non-Fructification of Karman

इति युक्तिभिरपि सिद्धं यत्कर्म ज्ञानिनो न सफलं तत्।
न ममेदमपि तु तस्येति दार्ढ्यतो न हि फलं लोके।। ६७।।

**67. Iti yuktibhirapi siddhaṃ yat karma
jñānino na spahalaṃ tat
Na mamedamapi tu tasyeti
dārḍhyato na hi phalaṃ loke.**

Trs.—The deeds performed by a wiseman do not bear him (the corresponding) fruit can (easily) be proved through logical (ratiocination) and reasoning (in the manner) a religious rite, performed with firm conviction in the world, does not bear fruit to the performer (of the rite) on account of it (having been) performed for the (welfare) of someone else.

Comment—This verse attempts to explain rationally as to why the deeds of a wiseman, which is to say of a selfrealised person, do not bear fruit for him. It is *a priori* asserted that a man who is steeped in the divine ocean of oneness has nothing more to attain or fulfill. He is so complete within that it is the delight of Fullness that brims over in all his activities, which, in the words of the *Gītā,* would mean that there remains nothing unattainable that he has to attain. As content and complete within, the yogi of this order performs deeds for the welfare of all, and thus his deeds do not bear any fruit. It would mean that deeds that are selfless, and are for the welfare of others, have no causal capacity to bear the fruit for the performer of the deed. In support of this viewpoint the author explains that the ritual action that is performed by the priest for the good of his client (*yajamāna*) bears no fruit for the priest. Similar is the case with the deeds of a self-realised person. A deed that is selfless does not have the power of moving the wheel of becoming.

68

Disengagement from Conceptual Cognition

इत्थं सकलविकल्पान्प्रतिबुद्धो भावनासमीरणतः।
आत्मज्योतिषि दीप्ते जुह्वज्ज्योतिर्मयो भवति।। ६८।।

68. Itthaṃ sakala-vikalpān pratibuddho bhāvanā-samīraṇataḥ
Ātma-jyotiṣi dipte juhvaj-jyotir-mayo bhavati.

Trs.—A (spiritual) aspirant who has (attained the state) of enlightnment (as a prelude) to self-realisation (and accordingly) has offered (the entire framework) of thought-construct (as an oblation) into the sacrificial fire of I-consciousness, which is lit by the (flowing) breeze of (absorptive) contemplation which (ultimately terminates in the realisation) of oneness with such fire.

Comment—The contemplative method that is prescribed in this verse pertains to the *śāktopāya* or with what may be called the Way of Energy. It is a Way in which the adept is asked, first of all, to visualise his consciousness in such a manner as if it would be identical with the fire that is burning in the sacrificial pit. It is in this pit in which are offered various kinds of materials as oblations in order to appease the benign as well as hostile forces. When an oblation is offered in the sacrificial fire-pit, it is consumed by the fire. Likewise in absorptive contemplation we are asked to offer our though-constructs as oblation to the blazing fire of consciousness, and it would be this illuminative consciousness that would devour them. Once differentiating factors like thought-constructs are so pacified as would allow the emergence of experience that would reflect the divinity of the self. Upon deepening this experience of being divine, there would spontaneously flow forth the non-dual experience of cosmic dimension, which would mean that the sense of differentiation would be completely devoured by the fire-like consciousness, and accordingly immersion in the non-dual consciousness would be experienced by the adept.

69

Freedom from Religious Discipline

अश्नन्यद्वा तद्वा संवीतो येन केनचिच्छान्तः।
यत्र क्वचन निवासी विमुच्यते सर्वभूतात्मा।। ६९।।

69. Aśnan yadvā tadvā saṁvīto
yena-kenacicchāntaḥ
yatra-kvacana nivāsī
vimucyate sarvabhūtātma.

Trs.—A person of wisdom, while wearing whatsoever clothes, eating whatsoever food, and living in whatsoever place, has the cognition of being the self of very contingent being, and (accordingly becomes) spontaneously liberated (from the bondage of unceasing *saṁsāra*)

Comment—A man of wisdom is highly regarded by the Trika system as being such a spiritual messanger who is not duty-bound to follow the scriptural injunctions or prohibitions of what one should do or not do, what kind of dress one should wear or not wear, or what kind of food one should eat or not to eat or where one should reside or not reside. Such a person is totally free from the restictive laws of religion. This condition is known as that of an *avadhūta*. He is free from the causal restrictions precisely because he has transcended the realm of difference and in terms of which he sees himself as being identical with the self of all. However, such a highly evolved person may not completely abandon the śāstric discipline for the purpose of maintaining social discipline. Whatever discipline he may follow, it is for maintaining harmony in society, and thereby preventing the ushering in of social anarchy.

70

Indifference Towards Sin and Piety

हयमेधशतसहस्राण्यपि कुरुते ब्रह्मघातलक्षाणि।
परमार्थविन्न पुण्यैर्न च पापैः स्पृश्यते विमलः।। ७०।।

70. Haya-medha-śata-sahasrāṇyapi
kurute brahma-ghātā-lakṣāṇi
Paramārthavinna puṇyairna ca
pāpaiḥ spṛśyate vimalaḥ.

Trs.—A yogin, who has rescued himself from (every form) of sin, (accordingly) has the possession of (such) knowledge that (contains nothing but) the Truth, (which at the same time denotes that) he remains so untouched both by righteousness and unrighteousness (as would remain unaffected) even if he performs horse-sacrifice by offering hundred-thousand (horses) or by committing countless killing of Brahmaṇas.

Comment—Deeds committed by a non-liberated person are causally so determinate as would terminate in the emergence of corresponding fruits. The fruit that comes into being is seen to be responsible in putting the wheel of becoming (*bhava-cakra*) into motion, and in terms of which the performer of the deed undergoes the process of rebirth. The state of rebirth depends on the kind of deeds one may have committed. A bound being, thus, is made to bear the consequences both of good and evil deeds. However, this determinate *karman*-causality is inapplicable in the case of a person who has won liberation from bondage. No action, whether good or bad, has any affect upon the liberated-one simply because his actions are free from the taint of selfishness. The liberated-one also recognises that he is not involved at all in the performance of actions; rather the divine forces through the instrumentality of his bodily organs perform whatever deeds are ascribed to him.

71-73

The Nature of the Liberated

मदहर्षकोपमन्मथविषादभयलोभमोहपरिवर्जी।
निःस्तोत्रवषट्कारो जड इव विचरेदवादमतिः॥ ७१॥

71. Mada-harṣa-kopa-manmatha-viṣāda-bhaya-lobha-moha-parivarjī
Niḥ-stotra-vaṣatkāro jaḍa iva vicaredavāda-matiḥ.

Trs.—(A person of highest spiritual realisation) may abandon (such moral deficiencies as) intoxication, joyfulness, anger, sexual drives, sorrow, fear, greed, delusion (as well as) may stop the (uttering) of hymns of praise, may cease to offer oblations into the sacrificial fire, may stop participating in discussions, while (at the same) may move about like a fool.

Comment—This verse explains that an authentic yogi overcomes all physical as well mental deficiencies like a true athlete, and while overcoming all the impediments, reaches his cherished goal. A yogi trains himself in such manner, while traversing the path of spirituality, as would make it possible for him to realise the state of contentment. The experience of spiritual contentment denotes that the yogi attains such a from of fullness of Being in which the physical and mental wants disappear like the coulds. Perfectly content within, a yogi does not feel any need for physical or psychological props—and the non-dual nondependence, discloses the nature of freedom. Upon realising full-fledged independence, a yogi totally frees himself from mental and physical wants. He does not make a show off of his spirituality or of his contentment, which is to say of his freedom, but looks like a fool to the one who has been deprived of such realisation.

मदहर्षप्रभृतिरयं वर्गः प्रभवति विभेदसम्मोहात्।
अद्वैतात्मविबोधस्तेन कथं स्पृश्यतां नाम।। ७२।।

72. Mad-harṣa-prabhṛtirayam vargaḥ
prabhavati vibheda-sammohāt
Advaitātma-vibodhas
tena katham spṛśyatām nāma.

Trs.—It is conceptual diversity which is (responsible) in giving rise to a class of emotions like intoxication, joy, etc. How and (in what manner) can such-like (emotions even be able) to touch a person who (is blessed) with the revelation of non-dual (wisdom)?

Comment—A true yogi who, upon experiencing Divinity at its core, empties himself completely of such human emotions that may become the cause for one's spiritual downfall. To experience downfall spiritually would mean subjugation to the becoming process of temporality, which would embody the principle of negation with regard to what one should not be. The yogi, thus, so empties himself of negative forces as would continue to be in the state of indifference, which would indicate not to be carried away either by emotions that are intoxicating or by emotions that are depressing. In the *Bhagavadgītā* such a state of indifference is termed as being the state of sameness or *samatā*. A yogi of the state of *samatā* is neither elated by pleasant experiences nor is he depressed by unpleasant ones. It is such a yogi who is referred to in this verse.

स्तुत्यं वा होतव्यं नास्ति व्यतिरिक्तमस्य किंचन च।
स्तोत्रादिना स तुष्येन्मुक्तस्तन्निर्नमस्कृतिवषट्कः।। ७३।।

73. Stutyam vā hotavyaṃ nāsti
vyatiriktamasya kiñcana ca
Stotrādinā sa tuṣyen-
muktas tannirnamskṛti-vaṣaṭkaḥ.

Trs.—(A self-realised person)does not have such an object to whom he could (offer) hymns of praise or adoration, and so he is (free form such acts as would embody) obesience (before a divine entity) or (would denote) the offering of oblations (into the sacrificial fire).

Comment—A person who has attained the state of liberation has no obligation to offer prayers before divine deities or pour in the oblations of clarified butter into the sacrifical fire-pit, which means that he is completely free from daily or occasional ritual acts. It further means that he is no more bound to follow, dogmatic or non-dogmatic, scripture-oriented injunctions and prohibitions. He is free from the performance of the ritual acts as well as from acts of adoration and worship on account of him having immersed in the ocean of divinity itself. Since the awareness of unity prevails insofar as sage is concerned, the need for worship and ritual acts disappears for him. For him the worship, the worshipper and the worshipped have become one, which means that there exist no more such entities as the worshipper, the worship and the worshipped. The sage, however, is not prevented from engaging in the acts of worship or prayer. It is upto the seer as to whether he prays or performs ritual acts. Usually the realised sages do pray in order people in general may not be misled.

74-80

The Vows of a Pāśupata *jñānin*

षट्त्रिंशत्तत्त्वभृतं विग्रहरचनागवाक्षपरिपूर्णम्।
निजमन्यदथ शरीरं घटादि वा तस्य देवगृहम्।। ७४।।

74. Ṣaṭṭrimśat-tattva-bhṛtam vigraha-racanā-gavākaṣa-paripūrṇam nijamanyadatha śarīraṃ ghaṭādi vā tasya deva-gṛham.

Trs.—Whether it be the body of a (sage) or of any one else—(all the bodies) consist of thirty-six *tattvas* (as well as are) equipped with (appropriate) outlets as windows (corresponding to) objects like pitcher, etc. (Whatever is emanated in the form of a body or object) can serve as a temple where (the sage may engage) in the act of worship and adoration.

Comment—Thus in one go is established that the entire manifest world is divine precisely because all the categories of existence have emanated from the Divine womb itself. Since every particle of dust is penetrated by the light of divine I-consciousness, it would mean that no phenomenal entity has the possibility to exist apart from consciousness. It is *citi* itself which reduces itself to the condition of finite objectivity, which consists of inert objects and conscious subjects. Thus all objectivity is characterised by Divinity, or should we say that objectivity is the expression of Divinity itself. If this is the case, it would indicate that every place or object or body is to be viewed as a temple where worship and adoration should flow spontaneously.

तत्र च परमात्ममहाभैरवशिवदेवतां स्वशक्तियुताम्।
आत्मामर्शनविमलद्रव्यैः परिपूजयन्नास्ते।। ७५।।

75. Tatra ca paramātma-mahā-bhairva-śiva-devatām sva-śakti-yutām Ātmāmarśana-vimala dravyaih paripūjayannāste.

Trs.—Therein (the yogi), while worshipping the Supreme Being as Divine Śiva in the form of Expansive Bhairava, along with his Divine Energy (deified as Śakti), makes the offering of (flowers) of self-contemplation (as a form of worship).

Comment—The worship of a yogi does not consist in offering flowers and other materials to a deity or to a divine representation conceived anthromorphically, which, according to Fuerbach, would denote transcendence of human characteristics that are imposed upon an assumed God. A yogi, on the contrary, transcends the conceptualised divinities by experiencing the Divine as being so pervasive as to be everywhere and it is for this reason that the Absolute is spoken of as being *mahā-bhairava.* This Bhairava is none other than his own self endowed with Divine Energy. It would mean that the Supreme Being in the form of I-consciousness reflects both luminous light and self-awareness, or, in the language of Tantras, Being as well as Becoming. The flowers that are offered in the divine temple of omnipresence are those of self-contemplation characterised by non-dual awareness in terms of which phenomena shine in the form shimmering purity, divinity and unity. It is a form of worship which falls within the rubric of Yoga of Knowledge (*jñānayoga*) or the Way of Energy (*śāktopāya*). The worship that is offered is as symbolic as would visualize the process of immersion of the contracted self into the ocean of the Supreme Self.

बहिरन्तरपरिकल्पनभेदमहबीजनिचयमर्पयतः।
तस्यातिदीप्तसंविज्ज्वलने यत्नाद्विना भवति होमः॥ ७६॥

**76. Bhahirantara-parikalpana-
bheda-mahā-bīja-nicayamarpayataḥ
Tasyāti-dīpta-samvijjvalane
yatnād vinā bhavati homaḥ.**

Trs.—The continuation of a *homa* (of the sage) is (dependent) on the heaps of grain of differentiation that apear conceptually in the form of external and internal objectivity (and which are) offered (as an oblation) into the fulminating (bright) and blazing fire of consciousness.

Comment—This contemplative procedure of offering conceptually-generated differentiation of external and internal objectivity as oblations into the bright and brilliant fire of consciousness is practiced by such yogis who follow the contemplative path of the Way of Energy. The heap of grain is made up of countless grains, and so the entirety of the heap of grain is seen as being the embodiment of diversity. It is the pervasion of such differentiation that is constitutive of phenomenal objectivity. Insofar as this conceptual as well as perceptual differentiation continues to be, there is going to be no relief from the pain and suffering that accompanies the cycle of rebirth. Trika system accepts the apparent reality of phenomenal diversity. It does not confine this diversity to the realm of conceptual or perceptual illusion, as is the case with Advaita Vedānta. However, this diversity is not as real as would constitute the heart of Reality. It can be transcended the moment we discover or recognise that we are basically divine I-consciousness, which is to say that we as embodied beings are but the contracted form of the Absolute. The moment we realise our identity with the Absolute, we become free from such conceptions which would impose upon us the limitations of finitude. One of the ways of removing or overcoming the sense of contraction is to follow the path of such contemplation as would enable the adept to offer the entirety of diversity as an oblation to the blazing fire of consciousness where it would be reduced to the nondifferentiating heap of ashes. As advanced Shaivayogin performs the *homa* so effortlessly as would lead to its continuous performance, and accordingly all the differentiating factors would be devoured by the fire of consciousness.

ध्यानमनस्तमितं पुनरेष हि भगवान्विचित्ररूपाणि।
सृजति तदेव ध्यानं संकल्पालिखितसत्यरूपत्वम्।। ७७।।

77. Dhyānamanstamitaṃ punar-
eṣa hi bhagavān victira-rūpāni
Sṛjati tadeva dhyānaṃ
saṅkalpālkhita-satya-rūpatvam.

Trs.—It is the divine Master itself who has (the power) and authourity of giving rise, within his intelligence, to this continuous and (wonderful) diverse objectivity—and this (emanation) becomes the incessant source of his meditation, (resulting thereby) in the emergence of conceptions concerning his essential nature.

Comment—This meditative practice also pertains to the Way of Energy. The yogin of this method does not engage in focussing his attention on some deity or on some nerve center. Such a form of meditative practice is followed by such yogins who follow the yoga system as enunciated by Patañjali. A Shaivayogin, on the contrary, does not engage in the attempt of suppressing the emergence of series of thoughts in the mind. The followers of Patañjali, on the other hand, will leave no stone unturned unless the chain of thoughts in the mind is eliminated. A Shaivayogin, instead, considers the rising of thoughts in the mind as being his own independent compositions, which is interpreted as being equivalent to the pure and divine nature of the Godhead. The rise of the chain of thoughts for a Shaivayogin results in such meditation as would enable him to realise the divine nature of the self. Thus there exists a contrasting difference between the Trika yoga and the yoga of Patañjali—the former adheres to the cataphatic view and the latter to the apophatic view, which is to say that one is affirmative and the other is negative.

भुवनावलीं समस्तां तत्त्वक्रमकल्पनामथाक्षगणम्।
अन्तर्बोधे परिवर्तयति यत्सोऽस्य जप उदितः।। ७८।।

78. Bhuvanāvalīṃ samastāṃ tattva-
krama-kalpanām-athākṣa-gaṇam
Antar bodhe parivartayati
yat so' sya japa uditaḥ.

Trs.—A *japa* (for an adept) is said to be (such a form of mantric utterance) in which (the practitioner), within his inward consciousness, turns around the entire sequence of the worlds (as well as) the arrangement of the categories or th grouping of the instrumental elements.

Comment—Ordinarily a *japa* is conceived to be the utternace of a mantric formula, and which is said to be of two types, vocal or silent. A vocal *japa* is uttered by using the vocal cords, whereas the silent *japa* is uttered mentally. This uttering of a *mantra* is accompanied by the counting of beads. A Shaivayogin, while engaging himself in the activity of *japa*, catches the hold of 118 worlds through the process of visualisation which is initiated in such a manner as if all of them are contained within his own I-consciousness. It is a process in terms of which the worlds, categories and elements are so made to dissolve into each other as would be realised perfect non-dual identity. It is the continuous repetition of *mantra* which ultimately results in experiencing the Reality as being one and single.

सर्वं समया दृष्ट्या यत्पश्यति यच्च संविदं मनुते।
विश्वश्मशाननिरतां विग्रहखट्वाङ्गकल्पनाकलिताम्।। ७९।।
विश्वरसासवपूर्णं निजकरगं वेद्यखण्डककपालम्।
रसयति च यत्तदेतद् व्रतमस्य सुदुर्लभं च सुलभं च।। ८०।।

79. Sarvaṃ samayā dṛṣṭyā yat
paśyati yacca saṃvidaṃ manute
Viśva-śamaśāna-niratām
vigraha-khaṭvāṅga-kalapanā-kalitām.
80. Viśva-rasāsava-pūrṇaṃ nija-
karagaṃ vedya-khaṇḍaka-kapālam
Rasayati ca yattadetat vratamasya
sudurlabhaṃ ca sulabhaṃ ca.

Trs.—(The person of spiritual insight) sees (whatever there is), which is to say, views everything as being homogeneous, (and accordingly) considers his I-consciousness as being everywhere (as a necessary place) for cremation-ground (where people reside). Viewing his own physical body as (a form) of skelton, he (the yogi) holds (simultaneously) a broken jar of objectivity (in his hands), filled with tasteful universal wine and (upon tasting it), he the yogin (watchfully) observes the wonderful Pāśupata vow, though easy (to follow), yet rarely (followed).

Comment—The yogi who has realised the non-dual truth concerning the Absolute is no more subservient to the differentiating thought-structures, and accordingly perceives and cognises everything as being of the essence of non-duality. The sense of difference totally disappears from the yogi, as the entire objectivity is made to melt in such way as to be as seamless as is the vast sky. Having realised the sameness of the whole, the sense of particularity with regard to one's body completely vanishes, and accordingly the body is given the same importance as would be given to a skelton, which would mean that the yogi dies to the temporal existence while still living physically. This sense of death prevails with regard to temporal existence, and it is symbolised by looking at the world as being nothing more than a cremation-ground. It is in this cremation-ground in which the finite existents reside. Ultimately this finitude of death is devoured by the flames of fire when the finite objectivity is offered to the living flames of consciousness. By devouring death, the yogi drinks the tasteful immortal wine of deathlessness in a jar that is made of bones. The transcendence of death is further enhanced when the yogi follows the Pāśupata vows, which consist of living in a cremation ground, wearing of a garland of human skulls, using a skull-bone-made-bowl to drink the wine of immortality, etc. Thus the yogi, on the one hand, visualises deathlessness through the representation of such symbols as, for example, wearing of skulls and drinking of wine in the skull-made-bowl, and, on the other hand, the principle of oneness or sameness is expressed in terms of vows. These vows, though may be simple, are rarely followed.

81-82

Perfect Unity as Fulfillment

इति जन्मनाशहीनं परमार्थमहेश्वराख्यमुपलभ्य।
उपलब्धृताप्रकाशात्कृतकृत्यस्तिष्ठति यथेष्टम्।। ८१।।

**81. Iti janma-nāśa-hīnaṃ paramārtha-
maheśvarākhyamupalabhya
Uplabdhṛtā-prakāśāt
kṛta-kṛtyas-tiṣthati yatheṣṭam.**

Trs.—Upon realising the Supreme Lord as being the basis of existence (as well as) devoid of beginning and end, the yogi reposes so contended (in himself) as he likes, (and accordingly such experience) comes to be due to the awareness of being such an experient.

Comment—It is the inner contentment that is the main feature of having realised the truth with regard to the Absolute as being devoid of beginning and end, which means that the Absolute is unborn, and thereby is deathless. Our experience tells us that which is subject to birth undergoes growth, sickness and death, which means that the object that is born has to die or perish one day on account its temporality. A yogi who has realised his unity or identity with that which essentially is unborn denotes the experience of one's own deathlessness, and thereby freedom from the becoming-process. Such an experience terminates in such contentment which is totally free from wants and lacks, and thereby from agitations and distrubances of desire. A person devoid of desire reposes perfectly in the tranquil awareness of the self.

व्यापिनमभिहितमित्थं सर्वात्मानं विधूतनानात्वम्।
निरुपमपरमानन्दं यो वेत्ति स तन्मयो भवति।। ८२।।

82. Vyāpinamabhihitamitthaṃ sarvātmānam vidhūtanānātvam
Nirūpama-paramānandaṃ yo vetti sa tanmayo bhavati.

Trs.—(It is *a priori* asserted that) it is the all-pervasive truth which, according to the above depiction, is seen as the self (or basis) of all existent entities (on account of it) having abandoned (all forms) of differentiating (factors), (and so is viewed) as being incomparable bliss. He who knows it (i.e. truth) as it is in-itself becomes it (namely, truth).

Comment—It must be clear by now that the Trika system of thought adheres to the philosophical standpoint which the Upnishads had already adumbrated. The Upanishads, however, lay much stress on the *prakāśa* aspect of the Absolute, thereby neglecting the *vimarśa* aspect. The Trika, on the contrary, views both the aspects as being the *sine qua non* aspects, which is to say that both *prakāśa* and *vimarśa* constitute the essential nature of the Absolute. It is this truth of the Absolute that makes it to be the all-pervasive basis or ground of existence everywhere. The *sādhaka* who has realised this truth of the Absolute as being the ground of his existence becomes the Absolute, which is to say that he now realises his deified nature. Prior to this realisation, the adept thinks of himself as being limited in every respect. Such a sense of contraction prevails due to being cloaked by such impurities as would terminate in blunting his vision of truth. Once the veil of impurities is removed, there thus occurs the revelation of such truth which establishes one's authenticity in terms of non-dual knowledge of reality.

83-84

Purity and Impurity

तीर्थे श्वपचगृहे वा नष्टस्मृतिरपि परित्यजन्देहम्।
ज्ञानसमकालमुक्तः कैवल्यं याति हतशोकः।। ८३।।

83. Tīrthe śvapaca-gṛhe eva
naṣṭa-smṛtirapi parityajan deham
Jñāna-sama-kāla-muktah
kaivalyaṃ yāti hata śokaḥ.

Trs.—A yogi becomes liberated when he has self-realisation (concerning his self as being non-different from the Absolute) and may (later on) abandon his body (according to his choice) at some sacred place or in the house of an outcaste (which is considered to be impure). (Whatever be the place of leaving the mortal body), the yogi attains the state of liberation (at any and every place), (thereby becoming) free from every kind of misery. Even if the yogi loses the sense of alertness (at the time of death), he is not (deprived) from the attainment of perfect liberation.

Comment—For a yogi who has gained the spiritual vision of sameness is no more subservient to the pulls and pushes of differentiation. For such a yogi, in the words of *Bhagavadgītā*, a cow, an elephant and a dog have an identical Being, which is to say, there exists no difference between an animal and a yogi insofar as essential nature is concerned. It is our physical form that makes us different. We are one and identical insofar as our divine nature is concerned. When seen from the point of view of sameness, there does not exist impure or sacred place. Every place is sacred because of it being the self-expression of the Absolute. Therefore, it has no significance for a yogi as to whether he dies in some so-called sacred place or in a place that is considered impure, like the house of an outcaste. As we are all of the same substance, so the demarcation of difference for the yogi disappears in the fire of consciousness. The other point that needs consideration is the persistence of alertness at the time of death. It is possible that a yogi may loose self-consciousness at the time of death. It does not mean that he is deprived of perfect liberation. A perfectly realised yogi—no matter what the physical state of affairs may be remains always a self-realised yogi on account of him having discovered his essential nature as being pure, divine and infinite. In the crucible of sameness every kind of difference is made to melt in such a manner as would lead to the attainment of oneness.

पुण्याय तीर्थसेवा निरयाय श्वपचसदननिधनगतिः।
पुण्यापुण्यकलङ्कस्पर्शाभावे तु किं तेन।। ८४।।

84. Puṇyāya tīrtha-sevā-nirayāya
śvapaca-sadana-nidhana-gatiḥ
Puṇyāpuṇya-kalaṅka-
sparśābhāve tu kiṃ tena.

Trs.—(Commonly the belief is held that those who pay) homage to the place (that is considered) as being sacred (gain the merit) of piety, while (on the opposite side it is believed that) death in the house of an outcaste terminates (in such a fall as would lead) to hell. Of what use would be both of these (points of view in the context of a yogi) who remains untouched equally by the stains of piety or unrighteousness.

Comment—Folk religiosity sometimes entertains such beliefs that run counter to spirituality. Of course, these common beliefs are not always illogical. It is natural to think that death in a clean place is preferable than in a place of dirt. But a yogi who has transcended the dualistic thought forms need not follow the way of life of common people. For him there is neither the sacred place nor the impure place. The concept of purity and impurity, merit and demerit, are reletive concepts, and so may be discarded when truth is known. The yogi, having known the truth, is no more touched either by good or by sin, since everything is assimilated in his own self.

85-86

Liberated while Living

तुषकम्बुकसुपृथक्कृततण्डुलकणतुषदलान्तरक्षेपः।
तण्डुलकणस्य कुरुते न पुनस्तद्रूपतादात्म्यम्॥ ८५॥

85. Tuṣa-kambuka-supṛthak-kṛta-
taṇḍula-kaṇa-tuṣa-dalāntra-kṣepaḥ
Taṇḍula-kaṇasya kurute
na punas tadrūpa-tādātmyam.

Trs.—Upon removing the inner and outer coverings of a grain of rice, (it loses the potentiality of sprouting which it had as a paddy seed). (If, however), the grain of rice is again covered with (the outer and inner) coverings it will never (posses the state of potency which it enjoyed) as a paddy seed.

Comment—The intention of the verse is to explain the state of a yogi, which emerges upon the removal impurities, which is to say that the pure and divine state of a yogi is like that of a grain of rice whose inner and outer coverings have been removed. As the grain of rice is incapable of sprouting again, likewise the yogi is no more subject to the processes of causal determination of becoming. It means that the yogi can no more be tainted by the impurities of *māyā,* and so is totally free from the transmigration of rebirths. He is now totally liberated. His spiritual look is as shining as is the whiteness of a grain of rice.

तद्वत्कञ्चुकपटलीपृथक्कृता संविदत्र संस्कारात्।
तिष्ठन्त्यपि मुक्तात्मा तत्स्पर्शविवर्जिता भवति।। ८६।।

**86. Tadvat kañcuka-paṭalī-
prithak-kṛtā samvidatra saṃskārāt
Tiṣṭhantyapi muktātmā
tat-sparśa-vivarjitā bhavati.**

Trs.—Likewise when I-consciousness is (completely) separated from the (limiting factors) of *kañcukas*, it (i.e., I-consciousness) obtains freedom from (the debilitating) bondage (in such a manner) as would not be affected by them (namely, by *kañcukas*) while continuing its stay in the world (on account of) (*karman*-generated) impressions.

Comment—Applying the theory of removal of outer and inner coverings of a paddy seed, it is thereby asserted that the contracted consciousness (*saṅkucita saṃvid*) similarly realises freedom from the bondage of limitations upon the removal of the coverings of *māyā*. It amounts to saying that insofar as consciousness is restricted to the cocoon-shaped *māyā*, it will experience itself as being limited with regard to knowledge and action, which would mean that it can do a little and would know a little. In this manner is contracted consciousness deprived of its divinity. However, the contracted consciousness realises its essential nature only upon the removal of sheaths of limitation, which denotes the restoration of the unconditioned state of freedom. And this restoration of unconditioned state of freedom is interpreted to mean freedom from such bondage that is characterised by the transmigration of endless births. The removal of the sheaths is a *sine qua non* for the realisation of unlimited freedom.

87-88

Freedom from Adjuncts

कुशलतमशिल्पिकल्पितविमलीभावः समुद्गकोपाधेः।
मलिनोऽपि मणिरुपाधेर्विच्छेदे स्वच्छपरमार्थः।। ८७।।

87. Kuśalatama-śilpi-kalpita-
vimalī-bhāvaḥ samudgakopādeḥ
Malino'pi maṇirupādher-
vicchede svaccha-paramārathaḥ.

Trs.—Even though a jewel may be polished by the most dexterous artist, yet it does not show its (innate) glow when put inside an (enclosed) case. (The jewel, however), shines (spontaneously) when taken out of the (enclosed) case.

Comment—The purpose of this verse is to explain the experiential fact of life, which tells us that a shining object will have no capacity of throwing out its brilliance insofar as it remains hidden in an enclosed chest. Likewise an individualised consciousness will remain confined or restricted to the measure its essential nature, which is characterised by divinity, is wrapped by the sheaths of contraction. It means that the divine and infinite consciousness will remain concealed, and such concealment is termed in the Trika as being ignorance or impurity. However, the essential nature of consciousness would shed its luminosity the moment sheaths of limitation are removed by following the Trika procedure of contemplation. This concealment (*pidhāna*) of the essential nature is one of the fuctions of Godhead itself. Opposite to the power of concealment is the power of revelation (*anugraha*)- and both of these functions of concealment and revelation are operated by Paramaśiva itself.

एवं सद्गुरुशासनविमलस्थिति वेदनं तनूपाधेः।
मुक्तमप्युपाध्यन्तरशून्यमिवाभाति शिवरूपम्।। ८८।।

**88. Evem sadguru-śāsana-
vimalasthiti vedanaṃ tanūpādheḥ
Muktamapyupādhyantara-
śūnyamivābhāti Śiva-rūpam.**

Trs.—Upon having (won) the purified (state) of I-consciousness through (appropriate) instructions of a right preceptor, (the yogi) shines (in the form) of an effulgent Śiva, (and consequently) does not insert himself into an another body as an adjunct while discarding the existing one.

Comment—The cessation of the becoming-process of transmigration is realised upon the purification of the individualised consciousness from the dross of impurities. The malignancy of impurities is such as would make empirical consciousness fractious and so prone to division and difference both conceptually and perceptually. Whetever we perceive or cognise, it is in terms of contrast and comparision, which means that we, for example, differentiate a table from a chair. This differentiation is epistemic insofar as contrasting is concerned. It is also ontic when the beingess of a table is said to be different from the beingness of a chair. Thus all our knowledge, and thereby our mode of existing, is fractious because it is seen and lived through the prism of contrasting images of difference. It is this impurity of fractious aspect of empirical consciousness which the yogi removes, and in doing so wins the vision of non-dual unity of cosmic consciousness. This immersion of the so-called individualised consciousness in the ocean of cosmic consciousness results in the freedom from the cycle of rebirth. This form of liberation from rebirth is termed as being "disembodied liberation" (*videha-mukti*), which is to say that it occurs after death, and so is considered to be the final one.

89-91

Life-Situation at the Time of Death

शास्त्रादिप्रामाण्यादविचलितश्रद्धयापि तन्मयताम्।
प्राप्तः स एव पूर्वं स्वर्गं नरकं मनुष्यत्वम्।। ८९।।

89. Śāstrādi-prāmāṇyād
avicalita-śraddhayāpi tanmayatām
Prāptaḥ sa eva pūrvaṃ
svargaṃ narakaṃ manuṣyatvam.

Trs.—Really it was he (the person) who had, under the various identifications, constructed on the received impressions from the unmoving faith in the scriptures, etc., taken birth in heaven, hell and the human world.

Comment—The determinate factor that determines the future course of life is rooted in the impressions whose scaffolding is derived from the kind of beliefs that one entertains with regard to one's faith. The source of this lies in the sacred scriptures that are revered as being the embodiment of divine revelation. It is the type of religiosity, based on scriptures, that generates the impressions, which in turn give rise to the superstructure, and in terms of which the nature of the future is determined. The impressions are as formative as would terminate into one's birth in heaven, hell or in the human world. Should we say that the impressions determine one's genetic code, and it is this genetic code that determines the state of future existence in terms of which an existent is made to experience whatever is built in the code. The nature of the code is solely dependent upon the impressions that we store within the code. It is the impression that determines our *karman,* and *karman* functions in the form of determinate causality. It is, thus, we ourselves who are responsible of what we are.

अन्त्यः क्षणस्तु तस्मिन्पुण्यां पापां च वा स्थितिं पुष्यन्।
मूढानां सहकारिभावं गच्छति गतौ तु न स हेतुः।। ९०।।

90. Antyaḥ kṣaṇastu tasmin puṇyāṃ
pāpāṃ ca vā sthitiṃ puṣyan
Mūḍhānāṃ sahakārībhāvaṃ
gacchati gatau tu na sa hetuḥ.

Trs.—When the last moment of life (is approaching death), there arises the condition that is either (full) of piety or (full) of sin. (And this existing condition subsequently) becomes the necessary cause for the type of rebirth for a deluded person. (However, this condition) is incapable of being the cause of rebirth (insofar as) a man of wisdom is concerned.

Comment—Apart from *karman* and impressions, the condition that prevails at the time of death is said to be one of the causes for rebirth. The condition of the last moment of life can either be one of righteousness or unrighteousness—and such a state emerges due to what we have been doing throughout life. The consciousness of a man of righteousness will have such a rebirth in terms of which he may fullfill his pious inclinations, whereas a person of evil mind may have such a kind of rebirth which may be troublesome and tormenting. It is the bundle of impressions that have the direct impact on our consciousness. Whose impressions are of good quality will generate such a state at the time of death that will be excellent. Equally will be evil impressions responsible in giving birth to a state that is full of wickedness. Subsequently one's birth will be either of good quality or of evil quality. Insofar as the man of wisdom is concerned, he is free from both the states, and thereby is free from the cycle of rebirth. It is so on account of him having recognised his essential nature, which is of the nature of consciousness and bliss, that there emerges the state of liberation.

येऽपि तदात्मत्वेन विदुः पशुपक्षिसरीसृपादयः स्वगतिम्।
तेऽपि पुरातनसम्बोधसंस्कृतास्तां गतिं यान्ति।। ९१।।

91. Ye'pi tadātmatvena viduḥ paśu-
pakṣi-sarīsṛpādayaḥ svagatim
Te'pi purātana-sambodha-
saṃskṛtas-tāṃ gatiṃ yānti.

Trs.—(There are some lower forms of existents like) animals, birds, snakes, etc, who, on account of having good impressions of error-free knowledge (of previous life), have the capacity of visualising the future course of their spiritual life (and accordingly) may move towards its realisation.

Comment—It is the contention of this verse that even the lower forms of existents are not completely deviod of thinking process. The process of thinking of such existents may not be as sharp as is of the humans, yet they are not as bereft of thinking as would have a vacuity of thinking. Some members of these species seem to have collected bundles of impressions of right knowledge, and so they make accordingly such effort as would uplift them from the present state of existence. It would indicate that living species of all forms have an innate tendency towards higher evolution. If this perspective is applied to a broader perspective, it would affirm Aurobindo's thesis that the world is evolving towards divinity, or what we may say that there is a twofold movement of ascent and descent. There is the ascent of phenomena towards divinity and the descent of the Divine towards phenomena. The immersion of the two into each other would usher in the process of transfiguration.

92-93

Rebirth and Liberation

स्वर्गमयो निरयमयस्तदयं देहान्तरालगः पुरुषः।
तद्भङ्गे स्वौचित्याद्देहान्तरयोगमभ्येति।। ९२।।

92. Svarga-mayo niraya-mayas-
tadayaṃ dehāntarāla-gaḥ puruṣaḥ
Tad-bhaṅge svaucityād
dehāntara-yogamabhyeti.

Trs.—(Depending upon the spiritual state), the existing (limited) self, while abiding in this mortal frame (called body), may have an association either with heaven or with hell. (In the context of the existing association) the self accordingly takes up (an appropriate) body upon the cessation of the present one.

Comment—The rebirth of an individual is determined largely by the present state of spirituality. The term heaven denotes such a form of spirituality that is so uplifting as to be transparent and pure. The term hell is the opposite of what the heaven stands for, which is to say that it designates a degrading form of life. A person who has evolved spiritually will have such birth that would be noble and encompassing, whereas the birth of a spiritually degraded person will be hellish, which is to say that such birth will be characterised by such experiences whose content is going to be tormenting. This is what these two terms imply.

एवं ज्ञानावसरे स्वात्मा सकृदस्य यादृगवभातः।
तादृश एव तदासौ न देहपातेऽन्यथा भवति।। ९३।।

93. Evam jñānāvasare svātmā
sakrid-asya yādṛgavabhātaḥ
Tādṛśa eva tadāsau
na dehapāte'nyathā bhavati.

Trs.—Likewise the shining of the self that (unfolds) at the time of self-realisation is for eternity (on account of it) persisting continuously, (which means that) even at the the time of death (this shining of the self continues) to be.

Comment—The shining of the self that eventuates at the time of realising the essential truth concerning the nature of the self as being non-different from the Absolute is not an occasional event but continues shining eternally. It is so on account of having accrued such error-free knowledge which never ceases to be even upon the cessation of the body as a living entity. The self is by nature luminous, and this liminosity is brought to the fore through the process of self-recognition, which means that the temporary veils of concealment are so removed as would not be possible for them to re-emerge. This conviction, in the form of impressions, gets ingrained within consciousness. It is this impression as conviction concerning the luminosity of the self that transcends time, and so lasts for ever.

94-95

The Behavioural Pattern of a *jñānin*

करणगणसम्प्रमोषः स्मृतिनाशः श्वासकलिलताच्छेदः।
मर्मसु रुजाविशेषाः शरीरसंस्कारजो भोगः।। ९४।।

**94. Karaṇa-gaṇa-sampramoṣah
smriti-nāśaḥ śvāsa-kalilatācchedaḥ
Marmasu rujā-viśeṣah
śarīra-saṃskārajo bhogaḥ.**

Trs.—Deficiency of (energy) of the group of sense organs, depletion of memory, breathing with effort, laxity of (bodily) joints and the (sickening) pain therein—all such (froms) of event are (considered to be constitutive) of bhoga, (which is to say) the ripening of the fruit of one's *karman,* (which is rooted) in the impressions (that have been formed) during one's physical life.

Comment—A man-in-the-street has the tendency of identifying his body with the self. This is one aspect of ignorance. The other aspect of it is in the identification of the body with the self. In either case the individual considers himself nothing else than the body. The deficiencies of the body are thereby wrongly imposed upon the self when, for example, it is asserted that I am feeling tired, I am tall or thin. It is such-like attributes that are wrongly identified with one's I-ness. It is like the imposition of the illusory snake on a real rope. In this misidentification rope is viewed as being snake, which it is not. Thus due to ignorance an individual being undergoes such experiences which do not pertain to him, ie, to the self. The events of birth, old age, sickness pertain to the body and not to the self. Upon gaining the state of right knowledge, the individual gains the power of discriminating the real from the unreal, and accordingly is won the ultimate battle against *saṁsāra* by becoming free from the becoming process.

स कथं विग्रहयोगे सति न भवेत्तेन मोहयोगेऽपि।
मरणावसरे ज्ञानी न च्यवते स्वात्मपरमार्थात्।। ९५।।

95. Sa kathaṃ vigraha-yoge sati
na bhavet tena moha-yoge'pi
Maraṇāvasare jñāni
na cyavate svātma-paramārthāt.

Trs.—In that manner is it possible for a man of wisdom to avoid the experience of reaping the fruit of deeds in the form of impressions of delusion while still living the life of the body? (Even while experiencing *bhoga*), he does not (allow the spiritual) fall to happen (insofar as) the divine nature of the self is concerned.

Comment—Whether one is a saint or a sinner, none can avoid the experience of reaping of the fruit of one's deeds. The causality of *karman* is as determinate as it would be an impossiblity to break the chain of its effect. It is upon completing the experiencing of the cycle of fruits of deeds that the determinate causality ceases to be. Insofar as *karman* fruit is conscerned, it has to be reaped; it cannot be avoided. While experiencing the fruit of a deed, the man of wisdom does not allow the spiritual fall to happen. No matter what the condition or situation may be, he always remains aware of his divine nature, which means that he remains as immersed in the self as to be constantly one with the Divine.

96

Instant Liberation

परमार्थमार्गमेनं झटिति यदा गुरुमुखात्समभ्येति।
अतितीव्रशक्तिपातात्तदैव निर्विघ्नमेव शिवः।। ९६।।

96. Paramārtha-mārgamenaṃ jhaṭiti
yadā gurumukhāt samabhyeti
Ati-tīvara-śakti-pātāt
tadaiva nirvighnameva Śivaḥ.

Trs.—On account of the fall of the extensively intense (divine) grace, the aspirant (subsequently) is initiated immediately by a (realised) guru in such a (spiritual) path that terminates (in the acquirement of knowledge) of the Absolute, (and as a result) the aspirant, without any obstruction, realises (perfect) non-dual unity with Śiva.

Comment—Whether it is concealment or disclosure of the divine nature, it is viewed in the Trika system as being a sport or play of the Lord. Equally is manifestation of the categories from Śiva down to earth termed as a play (*krīḍā*) of the Lord. The final playful act of the Lord is that of liberating the bound beings from the fetters of bondage by being as gracious and graceful as to send upon them the most intense form of grace. As a result of the descent of such grace, the aspirant immediately finds an appropriate guru who not only initiates him in the path of liberation-oriented spirituality, but equally imparts such scriptural knowledge as would be completely salvific. An aspirant on whom intense grace descends, he immediately obtains initiation in the *śāmbhava-upāya* or the Way of Śiva. The Way of Śiva is as highly prized as would result in the immediate realisation of non-dual unity with the Absolute. Those who follow this Way as a result of divine grace do not have to resort to any kind of ascetic activity. They just have to make use of their will in such a manner as would result in the immediate recognition of self as being divine, pure and infinite. Thus such self-recognition releases the aspirant from the last shreds of bondage. And liberation from bondage is characterised by such freedom that is devoid from the poverty of contingency. Insofar as one remains in the state of contingency, there will remain the poverty of deficiency or incompleteness. Thus our aim should be to realise the Fullness of Being and in terms of which the goal of liberation is realised.

97

Graduated Form of Liberation

सर्वोत्तीर्णं रूपं सोपानपदक्रमेण संश्रयतः।
परतत्त्वरूढिलाभे पर्यन्ते शिवमयीभावः।। ९७।।

97. Sarvottīrṇaṃ rūpaṃ
sopāna-pada-krameṇa saṃśrayataḥ
Para-tattva-rūḍhi-lābhe
paryante Śiva-mayī-bhāvaḥ.

Trs.—A *sādhaka,* while moving (spiritually) towards such situation as would be transcendent to everything, makes use of a ladder (of contemplative practice), and (in terms of which he ascends) the successive steps (in such a manner as would result) in the experience of unity with Śiva and (accordingly) the impressions concerning the Supreme Essence become fixed and deep.

Comment—This verse explains as to how the practice of the graduated path leads one to the ultimate spiritual experience of the Supreme Essence or of the Transcendent by ascending the successive steps, slowly and steadily, of spiritual ladder. It is a spiritual path that is determined by such grace which is of the nature of the middling (*madhya*). The aspirant, while following this path, ascends gradually the steps of the ladder in such a manner as would be consistent and regular. Accordingly the *sādhaka* reaches the final goal, which is to have the experience of non-dual unity with the Transendent.

98-102

Delayed Liberation of a Fallen Yogi

तस्य तु परमार्थमयीं धारामगतस्य मध्यविश्रान्तेः।
तत्पदलाभोत्सुकचेतसोऽपि मरणं कदाचित्स्यात्।। ९८।।

98. Tasya tu paramārtha-mayīṃ
dhārām-agatasya-madhya-viśrānteḥ
Tat-pada-lābhotsuka-cetaso'pi
maraṇaṃ kadācit syāt.

Trs.—Sometimes (it so happens) that a yogi, while desirous of attaining the highest (spiritual) state, takes rest in the middle of his spiritual (journey), and (accordingly) may die before reaching the highest (spiritual) state in the series (of states).

Comment—A yogi of this type who does not reach the intended spiritual goal functions under such form of middling grace (*madhya śaktipāta*) whose force is mild. It is the intensive form of grace (*tīvra śaktipāta*) that terminates in liberation that is immediate. In the case of *madhya śaktipāta* spiritual progress is graduated, and it may take more than one lifetime to reach the cherished goal of liberation.

योगभ्रष्टः शास्त्रे कथितोऽसौ चित्रभोगभुवनपतिः।
विश्रान्तिस्थानवशाद्भूत्वा जन्मान्तरे शिवीभवति।। ९९।।

99. Yoga-bhraṣṭaḥ śāstre-
kathito'sau citra-bhoga-bhuvana-patiḥ

viśrānti-sthāna-vaśād
bhūtvā janmāntare-Śivī-bhavati.

Trs.—A yogi who has a (fall while traversing the spiritual trajectory) is known as a *yogabhraṣṭaḥ* (in the language of the scriptures). (While not hitting the target, such a yogi while on the way) becomes the ruler of some (divine) abode (where he) enjoys the plentiful of pleasures. It is such an abode that (is used by the yogi) as a place of repose, and it is in the next life (in which) the yogi attains the state of Śiva.

Comment—A fallen yogi (*yogabhraṣṭaḥ*), according to the *Bhagavadgītā,* has his next birth in some reputed and righteous family. This assertion of the *Gītā* is equally supported by the Trika scriptures. While not succeeding in reaching the required spiritual goal on account of having some kind of fall, he is assured in his next birth that he will be so endowed with spiritual apparatus as would empower him to reach the goal of liberation. It is also possible that such a yogi may be born in some higher abode, may be in the abode of gods. Upon satiating himself with heavently pleasures, the yogi finally sets out on the path of contemplative journey in terms of which he realizes the spiritual goal of liberation. Accordingly the yogi attains both forms of liberation, namely, liberation-while-alive (*jīvan-mukti*) and disembodied liberation (*videha-mukti*).

परमार्थमार्गमेनं ह्यभ्यस्याप्राप्य योगमपि नाम।
सुरलोकभोगभागी मुदितमना मोदते सुचिरम्।। १००।।

100. Paramārtha-margamenaṃ
hyabhasyāprāpya yogamapi nāma
Sura-loka-bhoga-bhāgī
mudita-manā modate suciram.

Trs.—(This verse intends to depict the state of such a person whose longings for enjoyment are far stronger than for freedom from bondage). An adept, while having been constant and regular in the practice of the path of truth, fails to reach the height of contemplative spirituality, has (the possibility) of being born in some higher abode so as to enjoy there, with a joyful mind, the divine delights.

Comment—It is maintained that a temporal year in the life of a temporal existent is equal to one day of a being residing in the divine region. However, the length of a day could be hundredfold longer for existents who lead a deified life. If this is the case, it would mean that a Shaivayogin who would be a resident of a divine world would have the opportunity of tasting the divine delights for aeons. Upon being satiated, he no more hankers for divine pleasures. Instead he begins to tread the path of truth, which leads to the realisation of *mokṣa* or liberation. A Shaiva seeker of pleasures ultimately is so transmuted as to be a deified seeker of truth and in terms of which he is made to enjoy the delight of the truth of Freedom.

विषयेषु सार्वभौमः सर्वजनैः पूज्यते यथा राजा।
भुवनेषु सर्वदेवैर्योगभ्रष्टस्तथा पूज्यः।। १०१।।

**101. Viṣayeṣu sarva-bhaumaḥ
sarva-janaiḥ pūjyate yathā rājā
Bhuvaneṣu sarva devair-
yoga-bhraṣṭas tathā pūjyaḥ.**

Trs.—As the king of (great might) is revered by all the people of the kindom under his control, likewise is a fallen yogi worshipped by the existents of the divine abodes, which means that such a yogi does not loose spiritual lustre.

Comment—The spiritual glory of a fallen yogi does not diminish at all. It remains intact, and accordingly the beings of the divine realms offer their appropriate forms of worship to such a yogi.

महता कालेन पुनर्मानुष्यं प्राप्य योगमभ्यस्य।
प्राप्नोति दिव्यममृतं यस्मादावर्तते न पुनः।। १०२।।

**102. Mahatā kālena punar mānuṣyaṃ
prāpya yogamabhyasya**

**Prāpnoti divyamamṛtam
yasmādāvartate na punaḥ.**

Trs.—Upon the passing away of considerable period of time. (this *yogabhraṣṭa* yogi) takes anew a birth as a human being, (and accordingly) engages in such a contemplative practice as would result in the attainment (of the state) of immortality from which he (the yogi) never returns to the mortal frame of existence.

Comment—Upon the depletion of the store of meritorious deeds, the yogi is bound to return from the realm of the gods to the mortal frame of existence. It is the inexorable causl law, which says that the good deeds that one may have performed as a human being entitle one to be born in the heavenly world of Indra. The birth in a heavenly realm does not entitle one for liberation. A heavently being is entitled to have the taste of the immortal freedom from the bondage of rebirth only when he is born as a human being. It is as a human being that he engages in an appropriate form of contempletion, and as a result of this spiritual praxis, he is so empowered as to become immortal, which is identical with liberation from bondage, meaning thereby never to return to the mortal frame of existence. The Mahāyāna Buddhists have a similar theory with a slight difference. The *sādhaka,* upon death, enters Tuṣita heaven where he is provided with such a wherewithal as would empower him to immerse in the state of extinction, which is *nirvāṇa. Nirvāṇa* is such a state of cessation in terms of which no further becoming occurs, which is to say, there is complete freedom from the cycle of rebirth. In the case of a yogi the wheel of transmigration ceases to be upon immersing in the ocean of blissful consciousness.

103

Merits of the Knowledge of Reality

तस्मात्सन्मार्गेऽस्मिन्निरतो यः कश्चिदेति स शिवत्वम्।
इति मत्वा परमार्थे यथातथापि प्रयतनीयम्।। १०३।।

103. Tasmāt sanmārge'smin nirato
yaḥ kaścideti sa Śivatvam
Iti matvā paramārthe
yathā tathāpi prayatanīyam.

Trs.—Śivahood will (definitely) accrue to him whosoever, with right inclination, trudges upon this Path of Truth. While (considereing) this viewpoint, (an aspirant) must make (right) effort in following the path of *paramārtha,* (which is to say), the Path of Supernal Truth.

Comment—We are assured about the attainment of the ultimate goal of life, which is nothing else than the realisation of one's divinity in terms of which such cognition dawns as would affirm our identity with Śiva. The only proviso or condition that has to be fulfilled is that that we must make right and sincere effort of cultivating the supernal Path of Truth. For this purpose we have to surrender at the feet of a guru who not only is well-versed in the scriptural knowledge, but has himself realised non-dual identity with Śiva. It is from such a guru that we must seek instructions concerning the cultivation of the path of truth.

104-105

Diversity an Apparent Appearance

इदमभिनवगुप्तोदितसंक्षेपं ध्यायतः परं ब्रह्म।
अचिरादेव शिवत्वं निजहृदयावेशमभ्येति।। १०४।।

104. Idamabhinavaguptodita-saṁkṣepaṃ
dhyāyataḥ paraṃ brahma
Acirādeva Śivatvaṃ
nija-hṛdayāveśam-abhyeti.

Trs.—An immediate state of immersion/absorption is attained by the adept who contemplates on *brahman* in accordance with the brief description given by Abhinavagupta.

Comment—Instead of *samādhi,* it is the term *samāveśa* that is frequently used by the Trika school of thought to indicate the attainment of the highest non-dual spiritual state of identity with the Absolute. The state of immersion, though indeterminate, devoid of thought-constructs, is equated with liberation. The term liberation could be interpreted positively as well as negatively, depending on one's inclination and aptitude. Postively liberation is a *cataphatic* state in terms of which the taste of freedom is so savoured as to be indentical with immortality. Negatively it represents the *apophatic* state in terms of which is experienced the cessation of the pain-giving cycle of rebirth. It would be far more preferable if the term liberation is interpreted positively. Such an interpretation gives rise to hope and to the sense of contenment.

आर्याशतेन तदिदं संक्षिप्तं शास्त्रसारमतिगूढम्।
अभिनवगुप्तेन मया शिवचरणस्मरणदीप्तेन।। १०५।।

105. Āryā-śatena tadidaṃ saṅkṣiptaṃ
śāstra-sāram-ati-gūḍham
Abhinavaguptena mayā
Śiva-caraṇa-smaraṇa-dīptena.

Trs.—Upon meditating on the (lotus) feet of Lord Śiva, I, Abhinavagupta, became so illumined within (as to be able) to formulate a gist of the concealed essence of the *śāstra* in about a hundred verses in *arya* meter.

इति श्रीमहामाहेश्वराचार्याभिनवगुप्तविरचितः परमार्थसारः।

Iti-mahā-maheśvarācārya-Abhinavagupta-viracitaḥ Paramārthasāraḥ

Thus is concluded the *paramārthasāra* of the great *Maheśvara* teacher Abhinavagupta.

Glossary

Abhāsana, Appearance. Esoterically the term denotes emanation of objectivity.

Ahaṁ-bhāva, Feeling of I-ness.

Ahaṅkāra, The psycho-physical construct as ego, which is to say that, out of ignorance, the self is wrongly identified with the inert body or *prāṇa*.

Ahantā, I-consciousness.

Ajñāna, Ignorance is such knowledge that is erroneous or incomplete. It also denotes the identification of the self with not-self.

Akala, Such experient who experiences continuously the non-dual nature of the Absolute as being infinite, blissful, and perfect I-consciousness and at the same time containing the entirety of phenomena within itself. This kind of subject has its abode in the non-dual state of Shiva-Shakti.

Akhāyati, Ignorance

Akula, Śiva

Anantanātha, As Īśvara, God in relative sense, it descends to the level of *vidyā,* which is also known as Mahāmāyā. Anantanātha as God conducts the functions of godhead at the level of Māyā, and accordingly gives rise to *kañcukas, puruṣa* and *prakṛti.*

Aṇḍa, It is a particular division or sphere, which is said to be containing within itself a number of elements, thereby functioning as an external covering in terms of which the real nature of consciousness as Paramaśiva is concealed. As the number of spheres is said to be four, so accordingly the sphere of Earth is viewed as being the grossest covering; Prakṛti is termed as being the subtle covering; Māyā represents such covering that is more subtle than Prakṛti, and finally we have the sphere of Shakti, which is said to be the purest covering.

Aṇu, Aṇu is such an experient who is circumscribed by limitations, and on account of Māyā-generated limitations, the actions as well as knowledge of the individual being are also limited. He can know and do only a few things. Reduced to finitude, this limited being resides in the three impure spheres of Earth, Prakṛti and Māyā.

Anugraha, Such descent of divine grace as would incline a bound being towards the way of contemptation, and accordingly would lead him to self-realisation and in terms of which the goal of liberation from bondage is reached.

Anuttara, It denotes the highest reality, which is to say, Paramaśiva.

Aśuddha-vidyā, Knowledge that is impure, or should we say that it embodies the limited capacity of knowing of a limited being. It also is seen as being one of the limiting factors, or what is called *kañcuka.*

Ānanda-śakti, It embodies one of the five powers of God as well as denotes the blissful nature of infinite consciousness. This Power of Bliss mainly is predominant in Shiva-tattva, and Śakti-tattva is the result of it.

Āṇava-mala, It is on account of this impurity that an experient is reduced to finitude, and on account this finitude his capacity of knowing and doing is so circumscribed as would allow him to do only few things or know few things. This kind of impurity manifests itself in beings that are known as Sakalas and Pralayākalas.

Āvaraṇa-traya, The three impure coverings that conceal the infinite consciousness are the Āṇava-mala, Māyā and her *kañcukas* as well as the gross covering.

Bahirmukhatā, Externalisation of consciousness.

Bandha, State of bondage to which the embodied being is subject. It also represents such yogic practice in terms of which certain bodily organs are contracted and locked.

Bhairava. This term refers to the absolute Paramaśiva on account of it vomiting the categories out of itself, sustaining that which has been vomited, and resorping the categories into itself.

Bhava, It denotes the external as well as internal existence. It also refers to an object.

Bhāvanā, Such contemplative practice in which mantric formula is repeated *ad nausem* in such a manner as would result in the realization of truth. Such a method is made use of in *śāktopāya/jñānopāya.* Even in *āṇavopāya* contemplation as a technique for deepening interiorisation is used quite often.

Bhuvana, It refers to such an abode in which beings reside. It is maintained that there are, according to this system of thought, 118 such bhuvanas.

Brahman, It refers to such an absolute reality which manifests itself as phenomena.

Camatkāra, It explains such an experience of consciousness which is permeated by bliss. As an aesthetic exprience, it denotes the amazing artistic expression.

Cetanā, It refers to the Self as well as to Paramaśiva.

Cidānanda, Consciousness and bliss, which is seen to constitute the essential nature of the Absolute.

Cit, It denotes such aspect of consciousness which in itself is unchanging while being the substratum of change.

Cit-śakti, It is the primary as well as one among the five powers of the Absolute as consciousness. This power is predominant mainly in Paramaśiva, and subsequently gives rise to Śiva-tattva, which is seen as the substratum for Ānand-śakti.

Icchā-śakti. It embodies the power of will, and is considered to be one of the powers of the Absolute. It is a power which gives rise to such an urge within Paramaśiva that inclines it towards affecting the process of manifestation of objectivity. Accordingly are initiated the five processes of emanation, preservation, resorption, concealment and grace. This power of will is predominant in the Śakti-tattva, and accordingly manifests the Sadāśiva-tattva.

Idantā, "This" aspect of consciousness.

Īśvara-bhaṭṭāraka, The descent of Paramaśiva, in the form of an incarnation, to the level of Īśvara-tattva. He is considered to be the ruler of Īśvara-tattva, and is worshipped by the experients, called Mantreśvaras, who reside in this category.

Īśvara-tattva, It refers to the manifestation of such a category in which pure consciousness reflects in its own mirror, and there is appearance of objectivity in terms of "I am This."

Jagadānanda. It is such bliss of the Self which manifests itself as the universe, which, in other words, means of making divine bliss visible concretely.

Jāgrat-avasthā, The state of wakefulness.

Jīva, As bound being, a *jīva* is compared to an animal (*paśu*) on account of him having lost the sense of freedom. As a limited being, he is spoken of as *aṇu,* which is to say that he experiences limitations of every kind, whether it is with regard to knowledge or activity. A *jīva* also is equated with *puruṣa,* which means that he pertains to the category (*tattva*) called *puruṣa.*

Jīvan-mukti, A liberated person while still living in the physical body. While living in the body, he conducts the normal worldly activities in such a manner as would not in any manner taint him. He perceives the world and the hapening within it as a divine play.

Jñāna, A knowledge that is full, perfect and free from errors, and has the capacity of leading the seeker to the realization of truth.

Jñāna-śakti. One of the primary powers of Paramaśiva. It is through this power of knowledge that Paramaśiva visualizes within the entirety of phenomena that is going to be manifested externally. This power of knowledge is mainly predominant in Sadāśiva-tattva, and accordingly gives rise to Īśvaratattva.

Kalā-tattva, It embodies the limited capacity of an individual being to do only a few things.

Kāla-tattva, It embodies such an idea of time in terms of which it is interpreted as being characterised by succession. Time as succession would mean that the present event immediately trasforms itself into the past event while seizing the future event. In this manner the series moves on *ad infinitum.* Accordingly the finite individual being imposes this succession of time-scale on all the events that he may perceive or activities he may perform. It also denotes one of the *tattvas* of limitation. It is also seen as being one of the *kañcukas.*

Kañcuka-tattvas, It is maintained that there are five *kañcuka-tattvas* of limitation which veil the individual being in such a manner as to deplete his reservoir of freedom. The five limiting factors are *kalā, aśuddha-vidyā, rāga, niyati* and *kāla.* All these five *kañcukas* are the products of Māyā, which itself is considered to be the sixth limiting factor.

Kāraṇa, Cause

Kārma-mala, It is an impurity caused by our actions that are either good or bad. One of the signs of it is the emergence of an egoistic feeling in terms of which an individual considers himself as being the source of all his activities, which are being carried out through such instruments as the body, senses, etc. These actions leave such a deep impression as would terminate in the emergence of future birth, and thereby one is made to reap the fruits of one's deeds.

Kārya, Effect.

Kriyā-śakti, One of the primary powers of God. It is through this power that Paramaśiva externalizes the entirety of objectivity as being different from himself, which, in fact, is nondifferent when existing within him in a latent state. It is in the Īśvara-tattva in which *kriyāśakti* shines predominantly. It gives rise to the Vidyā-tattva and to the subsequent *tattvas* when it externalizes itself.

Kula, Śakti.

Kulāmanya, Śākta school of thought.

Madhya, Suṣumṇā or the central channel.

Mahā-māya, The lowest plane of Śuddha-vidyā. It is presided over by Anantanātha. Beings of this plane, although thinking of themselves as being of the nature of pure and infinite I-consciousness, yet at the same time consider everything to be subject to factors that constitute differentiation.

Mala, It embodies such impurity as would conceal the non-dual and divine nature of the self.

Mala-trayam. The triad of impurities, namely, Āṇava-mala, Māyīya-mala, and Kārma-mala.

Mantra-experients, such experients of the Mantra plane who are covered only by one impurity, namely, by the impurity of Māyā, which is characterized by difference.

Mantra-maheśvaras, Experients of the plane of Sadāśiva-tattva who are dominated by the awareness, "I am This."

Mantreśvaras, Experients of the plane of Īśvara-tattva whose awareness consists of the statement, "This is myself."

Māyā-tattva, It is the first impure category that owes its existence to Paramaśiva. It is such a category that serves the source for subsequent seven inert and impure categories, which are five *kañcukas, prakṛti* and *puruṣa.*

Māyā-śakti, It is such a divine Power of the Godhead through which is enacted the play of manifestation of categories from Sadāśiva to Earth. While engaged in manifesting objectivity, the Absolute as Godhead remains untouched by it.

Māyīya-aṇḍa, It is such a plane of Māyā in which are contained the *kañcukas, prakṛti* and *puruṣa.*

Mūla-prakṛti. The root-substance which serves as the material cause for the instrumental and objective elements. It also denotes the proper equilibrium among the three constitutents or *guṇas*.

Nirvṛti-śakti, It is identical with Ānanda-śakti.

Niyati-tattva, One of the *kañcukas* representating the natural law of causation, which operates within the realm of phenomenon. As a category of limitation, it binds experients through causation in such a manner as to make them to function in a restricted way.

Pañca-kṛtya, Five activities of the Godhead, and they are emanation, preservation, resorption, concealment and grace.

Pañca-śakti, Five primary powers of Paramaśiva, which are, *cit, ānanda, icchā, jñāna,* and *kriyā.*

Para-brahman, The metaphysical Absolute that is seen as having godhead as its fundamental nature. It is such an infinite and absolute reality that is of the form of consciousness. It is the congealment of the absolute consciousness that results, as it were, in the formation of objectivity in the manner of a reflection.

Paramārtha, The metphysical Absolute. It also denotes the essence of truth/reality.

Paramārtha-mārga. The path of truth that terminates in the realization of the non-dual truth of the Absolute.

Paramaśiva, Such reality as would allow the emanation of thirty-six *tattvas* as well as their resorption. It embodies such reality as would be infinite, all-encompassing, blissful consciousness, aware of itself as being divine.

Para-tattva, Paramaśiva, who is identical with the Absolute.

Parthiva-aṇḍa, It is a sphere representing gross form of matter. It is seen as being the most gross covering of I-consciousness consisting of Earth. It also denotes the Nivṛtti-kalā.

Pāśa, such fetters that cause bondage to be.

Paśu, A bound being who is fettered by such chains as finitude, differentiation and by good or sinful actions. As such this bound being becomes the victim of endless transmigration.

Pati, The entire ontological order consists of Lord, which is Śiva, Škati and Nara.

Pidhāna-kṛtya, Such activity of Paramaśiva that results in the concealment of his essential nature. On account of obscuration, bound beings lose interest in the study of scriptures and in the practice of spirituality. As a result of this activity of God, limited beings are pushed deeper into the regions of bondage.

Prajñā, It is a dreamless state (*suṣupti*) of a bound being.

Prakāśa, It denotes the essential nature of consciousness as being light, and in terms of which the existence of consciounsess becomes self-evident and which also empowers the objects that come into its contact.

Prākṛta-aṇḍa, The sphere that consists of root-substance as well as of its products, which are finer in nature. The categories that are found in this sphere are from *mūla-prakṛti* to water.

Pratibimba-nyāya, The theory that explains as to how reflection appears.

Pratibimba-vāda, It is a theory that explains the reflectional nature of manifestation of the universe.

Pratyabhijñā, The philosophical theory as to how to recognize one's forgotten essential divine nature.

Rāga-tattva, Restricted attachment for a perticular object. Consequently the knowledge that results from such attachment is also limited. It also denotes one of the *kañcukas.*

Rajas, one of the constituents representing passion, motion and activity.

Sadāśiva, The third pure category. At this stage of manifestation it is the experience of I-ness that is more prominent than Thisness. It is also termed as *sadākhya* on account of positing beingness (*sad*) at this stage. It is will or *icchā* that is prominent at the stage.

Śākta-aṇḍa, A plane that pertains to Śakti and contains within its ambit three categories of Sadāśva, Īśvara and Śuddha-vidyā. They embody the finer veiling of infinite consciousness.

Śakti, Energy or power of Paramaśiva.

Śakti-cakra, The collective whole of energies, or the wheel of twelve divine energies of the Self.

Śakti-daśā, It represents the absolute non-dual unity of two categories, namely, Śiva and Śakti.

Śakti-pañcaka, The five powers or energies of Paramaśiva, namely, *cit, ānanda, icchā, jñāna* and *kriyā.*

*Śakti-pāta,*Descent of divine grace.

Śakti-tattva, Such a stage of manifestation which only represent the intention or intent for manifestation of objectivity. It is the second manifest category.

Śāktopāya, Constant contemplative practice concering one's essential nature as well as having right conceptual understanding of reality.

Śuddha-tattva, Such elements that are absolutely pure and these elements are Śiva to Śūddhavidyā and Mahāmāyā.

Sadāśiva-bhaṭṭāraka, Such divine representation of Paramaśiva who reigns over the Sadāśivatattva.

Sadāśiva-tattva, It is a stage in which the idea concerning the manifestation of objectivity is incipient and unclear, and accordingly the consequent awareness with regard to manifestation eventuates in terms of "I am This."

Sakala, A bound being who exists under the influence of three impurities, and gets caught in the cycle of transmigration. Thus such a bound being is compared to an animal or *paśu.*

Samāveśa, It is such a spiritual state in which individualized consciousness gets merged in the ocean of universal consciousness, thereby representating the experience of absolute nonduality.

Saṁhāra, Dissolution or absorption. It is such an activity of Paramaśiva in terms of which certain manifest categories are reduced to their pre-manifest state, which is to say to their potential state.

Spanda, It is such a philosophical principle in terms of which consciousness is said to be constatntly pulsating or throbbing. It is on account of this throbbing that the Absolute as consciousness is enabled to manifest itself both inwardly and outwardly. It is through the external manifestation that the five divine activities of emenation, preservation, resorption, concealment and revelation are expedited.

Sṛṣṭi, It is such a divine activity in terms of which is vomited the external phenomena, which, prior to its manifestation, exists non-differently from the universal consciousness.

Sthiti, such divine activity which engages in the preservation of what has been manifested, and accordingly the cosmos is run in accordance with the natural causal law called *niyati.*

Suṣupti, The state of deep sleep.

Svapna, It is a state of dreaming, of deep thinking, meditating. etc.

Svātantrya, it is a philosophical concept which explains that the Absolute is totally free, nondependent, and so, without depending on anything, exhibits the five divine activities of emanation, preservation, resorption, etc. Thus the Absolute, out of its own free will, projects the entire objectivity on its own screen.

Taijasa, Denoting an existent in the dream state.

Tamas. One of the constitutents of *prakṛti,* representing sloth, darkness, inertia.

Tanmātras, The five undifferentiated subtle objects of five senses, and they are *śabda, sparśa, rūpa, rasa* and *gandha.*

Tāntrika, A follower of Tāntric thought and practice.

Tattva, Beingness or essence of a thing; thatness; principle.

Trika A philosophical school called Trika Shaivism. It embodies the trinity of Śiva, Śakti and Nara.

Triśūla, It is trident representing the three divine powers of knowledge, action and will.

Turya, It is a state that transcends the three empirical states of waking, dreaming and sleeping, and accordingly is termed as being the Fourth. As a non-empirical state, it is equated with the revelation of the self.

Turyātīta, It is such a transcendent state that transcends even the Fourth.

Udāna, Ascending breath as well as representing such yogic practice in terms of which Śakti is made to enter into the Suṣumṇā at the time of spiritual awakening.

Unmīlana, unfolding of manifestation.

Upādāna, Material cause.

Upādhi, limiting adjunct.

Vācaka, word or indicator.

Vācaya, The indicated or the object.

Vaiṣṇava, A follower of Vaiṣṇava school of thought.

Vidyā, One of the *kañcukas* representing knowledge that is limited.

Vijñānākala, An experient below Śuddha-vidyā but above Māyā. He is such an experient who possesses awareness but is devoid of activity.

Vimarśa, It embodies self-awareness of the Absolute in terms of the fullness of knowledge and action, and accordingly is affected the manifestation of objectivity.

Viśva, Beings in the waking state.

Viśvottīraṇa Transendent.

Yoga, A contemplative school that prescribes inward way of reaching the transcedent goal. It also embodies the state of union between the worshipper and the worshipped.

Yoga-bhraṣṭa A yogi who dies before reaching the goal.